All Things Herriot

James Alfred Wight (James Herriot) treating a horse.
Courtesy *Northern Echo*.

All Things
HERRIOT

*James Herriot and His
Peaceable Kingdom*

Sanford Sternlicht

SYRACUSE UNIVERSITY PRESS

Copyright © 1995 by Syracuse University Press
Syracuse, New York 13244-5160
All Rights Reserved

First Edition 1995
95 96 97 98 99 00   6 5 4 3 2 1

The paper used in this publication meets the minimum requirements of
American National Standard for Information Sciences—Permanence of
Paper for Printed Library Materials, ANSI Z39.48-1984. ∞™

Library of Congress Cataloging-in-Publication Data
Sternlicht, Sanford V.
　　All things Herriot : James Herriot and his peaceable kingdom /
Sanford Sternlicht.
　　　p.　cm.
　　Includes bibliographical references (p.) and index.
　　ISBN 0-8156-0322-3 (cl)
　　1. Herriot, James.　2. Herriot, James—Influence.　3. Popular
culture.　I. Title.
SF613.H44S74　1995
636.089′092—dc20　　　　　　　　　　　　　　　94-39523

Manufactured in the United States of America

To Joan Eyeington of York, my friend for thirty years; and to the memory of my friend Dave Eyeington (1892–1990), joiner of York, and once corporal, Fifth Battalion, West Yorkshire Regiment, France, 1915–1918.

Sanford Sternlicht is part-time professor of English at Syracuse University and a poet, critic, and theater director. His works of criticism include *John Webster's Imagery and the Webster Canon* (1972), *John Masefield* (1977), *C. S. Forester* (1981), *Padraic Colum* (1985), *John Galsworthy* (1987), *R. F. Delderfield* (1988), and *Stevie Smith* (1990). He has edited *Selected Short Stories of Padraic Colum* (1985), *Selected Plays of Padraic Colum* (1986), *Selected Poems of Padraic Colum* (1989), and *In Search of Stevie Smith* (1991) for Syracuse University Press.

Contents

Illustrations

Preface

Millions of people, young and old, the world over, love James Herriot. He is their friend. They feel they know him as one might know an uncle or a neighbor. They wish they had a doctor like him, one who really cares and makes house calls. They are more familiar with "his" life than they are with the lives of their political leaders. I have placed quotation marks around the word *his* because there is no retired Yorkshire veterinarian and writer named James Herriot. The name is a nom de plume. It is also safe to say that no one improbably named Siegfried Farnon ever lived. The true author is James Alfred Wight, who is a retired veterinarian and active writer approaching the age of eighty. How James Herriot came into being and how the "memoirs" of that constructed narrator, through cross-fertilization, became a darling of popular culture and a multimedia financial milk herd are two of the subjects of this book.

The third subject is an appreciation of a fine literary craftsman, "Alf" Wight, who has shaped the material of his ordinary, useful, relatively uneventful life in the north of England during the middle of the twentieth century into a series of engrossing books that have given great pleasure to vast numbers of people and have helped the cause of respect for, and kind treatment of, animals more than any other artistic endeavor since Walt Disney's *Bambi*.

All Things Herriot: James Herriot and His Peaceable Kingdom is the first full-length study of this best-selling author, whose work, adapted for TV, has swept through the world in one of the most popular and enduring series of all times: *All Creatures Great and Small*. My text offers a comprehensive, up-to-the-moment evaluation of the Herriot achievements, and it offers the most detailed biography of James Alfred Wight in print to date. I hope that it will add to the pleasure of entering and to the understanding of "James Herriot's Peaceable Kingdom."

I am grateful for the generous permission of St. Martin's Press to quote from *All Creatures Great and Small, All Things Wise and Wonderful, All Things Bright and Beautiful, The Lord God Made Them All, Every Living Thing,* and *James Herriot's Yorkshire*.

Several people have helped with this book and I thank them all, especially Edward Bermudez, Amy Fischman, Kristin Gaugler, William D. West, and the interlibrary loan staff of Bird Library, Syracuse University.

Syracuse, New York   Sanford Sternlicht
June 1994

All Things Herriot

1

The Prince of the Peaceable Kingdom

Surely the planet's best-known veterinarian is "James Herriot," the pen name of James Alfred Wight. Although his works are listed by the Library of Congress under Veterinary Science, it is as a memoirist that he has caught the popular literary imagination of much of the reading world and achieved an international audience of tens of millions of readers. The books have been translated into more than a dozen languages, and the readers span ages nine to ninety. Two feature-length films and a BBC television series have solidified Herriot's hold on his public. The BBC TV series, begun in 1978, and titled "All Creatures Great and Small" though derived from three of his books—*All Creatures Great and Small* (1972), *All Things Bright and Beautiful* (1974), and *All Things Wise and Wonderful* (1977)—has created a powerful visual image of pre–World War II rural Yorkshire, frozen in time through perpetual reruns around the globe.

That Yorkshire of Herriot's memory and imagination is a prelapsarian paradise, a peaceable kingdom, a snowcapped Eden, where humans and domesticated beasts live in gentle harmony and where society functions smoothly under the aegis of Judeo-Christian values, the Protestant work ethic, a Roman Catholic emphasis on works and acts, and traditional British civilities derived from class stasis, in the ever-receding, simpler world of our agrarian ancestors. Generations of Herriot readers

1

and viewers are waiting to be born, to enjoy what Lionel Tiger would call the ideopleasures of Herriot's texts, and to visit with mind and body the lost kingdom of Herriotland.

The context of acclaim is always of interest and importance in understanding mass acceptance of cultural iconolatry. Operative in the case of the Herriot memoirs is a comfortable modernistic confirmation of popular assumptions, such as the altruism and wisdom of healers; the fidelity of mute beasts; the integrity of agricultural workers created by a hard but just nature as they engage in the archetypal struggle of life on the land; the harmlessness of a little drinking and juvenile prankishness; and the structuring support of conventionality, all superimposed on an inner psychological dynamic of modernism: the elevation of the gentle heroes, the Little Tramps, the Schweiks, and the physician protagonists of Somerset Maugham, A. J. Cronin, 1930s and 1940s films, and 1950s TV programs such as *Marcus Welby*.

The essential drama of the Herriot memoirs is the symbolic reenactment of the physician's combat with death. That drama is an immortal passion play far older than its early appearance in the tales of Sinuhe the Egyptian. It reaches into our unconscious minds because humans beset with pain and fear, seeking the salvation of the body, have always invested hope in healers of both the physical and faith varieties. Also, within Herriotland the human struggle against death is transferred from people to animals, but it is really about us, our love of life, especially our own, and our need for compassionate and successful healers. Efficacious for conveying this drama are Herriot's basic direct narrative style and his wise stylistic decision to provide satisfying expectational closure. The Herriot genius is his Aesop-like ability to make inarticulate people and animals "speak" eloquently through gratitude, affection, pain, anger, or other means.

The protagonist James Herriot, as modernist popular hero, is an antielitist humanist who lives in society; serves a close community of farmers as a bulwark in the primeval battle against diseases that could quickly destroy a way of life and livelihood; serves the dominant culture's cultural, religious, and political values; goes to war without hatred to serve his country when needed; has small faults and a minor vice, a liking for a little drink; is generous with his self; loves and courts as a prototypical twentieth-century bumbling male; marries; and fathers and raises two children. Despite living within an economy that exists and prospers to a large extent on the slaughter of animals, Herriot never ceases to wonder and thrill at the miracle of life.

His wife, Helen, is neither modern woman, flapper, nor "New Woman" of Edwardian vintage. She is the "Good Woman" of the mid-Victorian era, an archetypal mother-figure seemingly wiser and morally firmer than her husband, whom in fact she has chosen. She helps with the practice a little but serves primarily as household manager and ark of conscience and morality for her nuclear family and her extended family that includes for a time the fellow practitioners, Siegfried and Tristan. James, Helen, their family, their friends, and the people of Yorkshire are clearly a part of the human herd, and, pantheistically, of the totality of life.

The memoirs of James Herriot are a segment of what could be called postimperial British popular literature. For Britain, shorn of empire and singular international importance, Herriot's narratives offer opportunities for the public to look inward and backward, thus providing moments to ignore current economic and racial problems as well as contemporary inconsequentiality. For many members of the even larger American audience, the memoirs connect to a collective received memory of hardy nineteenth-century New England farming and a culture of unquestioned absolute ethical and moral values derived from direct contact and struggle with an instructive natural world. Thus, the memoirs, like most works of popular literature, hold a nostalgic mirror up to society to show it how it thinks it once was and, more significantly, how it would like to be if only circumstances were different.

.   .   .

When first viewing an episode of the BBC's *All Creatures Great and Small* series, Herriot fans were and are surprised that the actor Christopher Timothy, playing James, speaks without a Scottish dialect even though constant reference to his Scottish origin is made by his mentor and employer, Siegfried Farnon. The TV series is partially accurate, at least to the extent that the real-life James had English parents; however, the real-life veterinarian did have a noticeable Scottish accent when he arrived in Yorkshire and to this day speaks with a faint trace of a Glaswegan burr.[1] James Alfred Wight, the only child of James Henry and Hannah Bell Wight, professional musicians, was English-born on 3 October 1916, in the middle of World War I, in Sunderland, County Durham, now Tyne and Werr. The family moved to the Glasgow suburb of Hillhead three weeks after the birth of James Alfred, a child whom everyone called Alf. It should be noted that under what may be residual prenatal influence, Wight remains fanatically loyal to the Sunderland Football Club,[2] even though he resides in the partisan territories of Leeds and Middlesbrough.

Hillhead provided easy access to the amenities of a large city, but also to the beautiful hills of Scotland and to Loch Lomond. Alf spent much of his happy childhood and youth wandering the highlands with his dog; camping and climbing as he grew older. These experiences engendered in him both a love of animals and a deep feeling for nature, a wild landscape, and the countryside of Britain.

Alf grew up in a very musical household, joyful with his mother's singing and his organist father's piano practice. Mozart and Beethoven remain his favorite classical composers, but Elgar is special for him among the British. Wight's home was also full of books. As an only child he found recreation in reading and companionship in the volumes of his father's bookshelves. As was frequently the case with children of his generation, Wight began his reading with comic books, but soon shifted to adventure-writing authors such as H. G. Wells, Conan Doyle, and H. Rider Haggard. Throughout veterinarian Wight's long career in practice, reading has provided escape, solace, and relief from the exacting labor of his profession.

Wight attended Hillhead High School, a typical Scottish municipal educational institution of the time with a traditional emphasis on character building and discipline. Although generally enjoying high school, Wight, like many boys, did not enjoy the disciplinary aspects of his educational experience. He saw much that was either humorous or ludicrous in his classes and was prone to laughing aloud during solemn pedagogical moments, resulting, as was the custom in Scottish schools at that time, in regular corporal punishment consisting of strokes with a leather belt kept handy by stern schoolmasters. But the masters were competent teachers and the education of a very high quality. Wight holds no grudge but, rather, appreciates how instruction and discipline helped prepare him for life and a career, despite the fact that his science scores were relatively poor.

Wight was always an animal lover, but at the age of thirteen he read in *Meccano Magazine* an article on the life of a veterinarian, entitled "Veterinary Surgery as a Career," and on the spot dedicated himself to career in veterinary science.

After high school, and still strongly committed to a life as a veterinary surgeon, Wight managed to be accepted into the excellent Glasgow Veterinary College, despite his less-than-outstanding high school record. Wight worked hard in veterinary school, hoping and planning to treat domestic animals as a small animal surgeon in his own well-equipped, completely up-to-date hospital after qualifying as an M.R.C.V.S., but he graduated in 1937 into the Great Depression, and most of his classmates were unable to find any work in their profession. Some took jobs working on the docks and in the shipyards of Clydeside. Still hoping for a life with cats, dogs, parrots, and guinea pigs, Wight answered a newspaper advertisement for an assistant veterinarian in the small Yorkshire town of Thirsk.

Growing up in the Glasgow environs, Wight had never considered a life in a place like the Yorkshire Dales and North Moors with its rugged farmers surviving on cattle, sheep, pig raising, feed crops, and vegetables; its challenging climate; and most of all, its stunningly beautiful, though often wild and desolate, landscape. It is the Pennines that form the chief architectonic for the Herriot books. They are omnipresent, shaping the lives of all that live on the hills and in their shadows.

Wight received the job in Thirsk and became assistant in the established practice of Veterinarian Donald V. Sinclair, the exotically named Siegfried of the memoirs. Wight would spend his entire working career in this one practice and in this one locale. Surely few persons have ever more truly found their vocation. He came to Yorkshire knowing nothing about agriculture and little about herd economy. Furthermore, the life was much harder than he had anticipated. Wight later said: "The life of a country vet was dirty, uncomfortable and dangerous."[3] His work was primarily with large farm animals: calving cows, castrating bulls, pigging sows, lambing sheep, and foaling mares, although family pets did constitute a part of the practice. Wight was and is a soft-spoken, gentle man, often on the defensive with the rough, outspoken Yorkshiremen who were his chief clients. But he said of the work: "I loved it. Some of the customers thought I was a pretty fair vet, others regarded me as an amiable idiot, a few were convinced that I was a genius and one or two would set their dogs on me if I put a foot inside their gates."[4] As with any healer his life was full of exhilarating successes and depressing abject failures.

In 1939 Wight took on the additional responsibility as a veterinary inspector for the United Kingdom Ministry of Agriculture, Fisheries, and Food. As a reasonably ambitious man of twenty-three, Wight expected to find other opportunities opening up in his career and to move on to other locales in the course of constructing that career, but early on in his Yorkshire sojourn, elements of his existence and environment began to seep into his subconscious, to solidify, to construct a foundation of belonging and permanence. Slowly, he came to feel that he could not happily spend his life away from the high and windy land; from the sweet smell of growing things; from the dramatic changes of season; from the wind and the rain; from the strong, taciturn, stoic, good people of the land; from his eccentric but warm-hearted employer, soon to be partner; from the Georgian house, 23 Kirkgate, Thirsk (Herriot's Skeldale House; the BBC location is a house in Askrigg in the Dales), in which he worked and resided; and from the roots that were growing slowly and deeply from his senses into his soul.

A local farmer's daughter, Joan Catherine Danbury, Herriot's "Helen," caught Wight's eye. They fell in love. The pleasant bachelor life with Donald Sinclair and Donald's younger brother Brian Sinclair (Herriot's "Tristan") no longer seemed so appealing, and Joan and James were married in November 1941 at St. Mary Magdalene's Church, Thirsk. On their wedding day, Donald Sinclair made Wight a partner in the practice, to be remembered in the dales and on the moors as Sinclair & Wight. In that labor-short wartime, the newly-weds spent their honeymoon working together, performing tuberculin tests on herds of cows. For the first eight years of their marriage, with Joan working as a secretary in a mill for some of the time,[5] the young couple lived on the third floor of the surgery residence, in rooms furnished from second-hand, rummage, and house sales. James was available for night calls, and Joan kept the books for the practice. Their children, both born in the Sunnyside Nursing Home on The Green in Thirsk, were educated in the Thirsk School.[6]

Veterinary practice in pre-sulfonamides and pre-antibiotics days was often hit and miss, depending on the experience and the talent of the veterinarian to diagnose animal ailments and prescribe treatments that often had not changed in a century. The pharmacology seems exotic today: Tincture of Camphor, Formalin, sugar of lead, Album, Perchloride of Mercury, emetics, diuretics, and anesthetics. Enemas were also common. Exercise was often prescribed for a variety of ailments, with the result, quite predictable of course, that the animal quickly improved or died. Wight himself discovered that putting an extremely ill or hurt beast to sleep for a couple days, and allowing the "patient's" constitution to work on itself without the stress and terror of pain, had efficacious results.

When World War II broke out in September 1939, Wight's work as a veterinarian helping with vital agriculture at first put him in the military category of "Reserve Occupation," and so he was not conscripted for military service in the war, but, for honor, manhood, and love of country, he volunteered for the Royal Air Force in 1943 and was called up on his twenty-seventh birthday. It was excruciatingly difficult for Wight to leave his adored young wife, the peaceful countryside that he also loved, and the profession that gave him happiness and satisfaction. He served throughout the remainder of the war as an enlisted man and a pilot trainee, eventually soloing at the flying school at Windsor even though he was much older than almost all the other trainees. He somewhat regretted volunteering when he did, for not long after, veterinarians, including Brian Sinclair, were called in their profession and commissioned in the Royal Army Veterinary Corps. After all, it did not make a lot of sense for a veterinarian to be serving in the air force.

While he was on active service in 1944, and fortunately not shipped overseas, James went AWOL to be at Joan's side as she gave birth, attended by a midwife at the Sunnyside Nursing Home. Their son, born on 13 February, was christened Nicholas James, the "Jimmy" of the stories, and is today a qualified veterinarian and partner in the practice. Nicholas's birth was the first human birth Wight had ever witnessed, and he had to ask the midwife if the child was healthy.

Fortunately, Wight was not caught AWOL, but after qualifying as an aviator and on the verge of being shipped to the war on the continent, he was required to have an operation at the RAF Hospital, Creden Hill, near Hereford, for an old but recurring ailment, and upon recovery, and the war nearly over, he was medically discharged to return to the practice in Thirsk.

It was not until during the war that Herriot became fully reconciled to a practice consisting almost entirely of attending large farm animals. During his military service he longed for the roads, the hills, and the open country of Yorkshire, and he realized he did not want to be shut up in a surgery all day treating pets after all. He would pull over to the side of the road and ease himself down on the turf, close his eyes, and let the sun warm his face, while peaceful thoughts of Yorkshire made life seem very good indeed.

On 9 May 1949 Rosemary, the second and last Wight child, was born in the same room in which their Nicholas James had entered the world. Rosemary, like Jimmy, loved to make calls with her father, and, also like her brother, desired to go eventually to veterinary college and join the practice, but Wight paternalistically decided that the work was physically too hard for a woman, and so Rosemary went to medical school and now practices in Yorkshire too. Wight later somewhat regretted influencing his daughter to give up her dream of veterinary medicine as he came to realize that the burgeoning pet population of Britain created substantial opportunities for veterinarians to specialize exclusively in small-animal care.

The 1950s passed uneventfully for the Wights. Their healthy children grew up. The practice flourished. New medicines improved the treatment of both farm animals and pets. The horse nearly disappeared as a draft animal, replaced by the gasoline engine tractor. The lot of the Yorkshire farmer improved along with England's growing prosperity. Wight kept a diary of his experiences as a country vet.[7] It served as a reference for treatment, but he also enjoyed recording amusing or poignant incidents in his practice, family events, and the doings of his partners, as well as how he felt about life near the Pennines, in the beautiful natural world in which chance had set him down.

As Wight moved into his late forties, he grew somewhat restless, perhaps feeling that life in his beloved Yorkshire could be somewhat parochial and confining, and so he availed himself of two opportunities for travel and professional growth. First, in October 1961, he accepted a job as traveling veterinary attendant to a herd of pedigree sheep shipped from Hull to Lithuania, then a state within the Soviet Union and thus behind the Iron Curtain. Wight enjoyed the adventure, and two years later, in August 1963, accepted a similar position flying to Istanbul with a herd of forty cattle in a rickety Globemaster. This adventure, with its dangerous dénouement, is described in *The Lord God Made Them All.*[8] It seemed to cure Wight of his wanderlust. Instead, he turned inward to his diary and to the thought of serious writing.

Wight had often talked to Joan about writing. He felt that his life had been, and still was, interesting and full of touching and amusing incidents and that it would be worth recording and sharing with a reading audience. According to Wight, Joan was not impressed: "I kept telling my wife for 25 years that I was going to write a book, but she didn't think I would. Then one day she said to me: 'We had our silver wedding last week, and you're 50, you'll never do it now.' So I thought, okay mate, I will and I got started."[9] The children were grown, and the practice was doing well; there were no more excuses. He bought paper and taught himself to type.

Wight wrote in the evenings after a hard day's work, and he wrote into the night, often dragged away with a phone call to treat a sick animal, returning later to his typewriter by the TV set. But he was not satisfied with the results.[10] He quickly realized that having amusing stories to tell did not by itself make for creating artful narrative. He says that he "tried to write beautifully balanced sentences like Macaulay's Essays, but I soon realized that was no good. So I got rid of most of my adjectives and high-flown prose and thought how I would tell the tale in a country pub."[11]

Wight was also an avid reader, and now he began to study the authors he admired: Dickens, Conan Doyle, Robert Louis Stevenson, and Hemingway. For nearly two years he apprenticed himself, reading manuals of the "How to Be a Writer" and "Teach Yourself to Write," genre and he sent innumerable short story submissions to periodicals and the BBC, only to receive form rejections. Wight recollects: "There's a special noise that a rejected manuscript makes when it comes through the letterbox and it hits the doormat. A sort of sick thud. I got to hate the sound of it."[12] He came to dread dealing with the mail. The indifferent rejections were especially painful. He continued to study and experiment with his writing, and upon learning the art of the flashback from Bud Shulberg's *The Disenchanted,* he became determined to rework his short narratives into book form. After eighteen months of part-time labor, consisting of time segments as brief as thirty minutes and slipped in between patients or calls, he had a book, which he promptly sent off to a publisher recommended by a friend. Eighteen months later it came back rejected. It went out several more times. One publisher told him to rewrite it in the first person, but when he did so the manuscript was again rejected. Finally, he threw it in a drawer, but Joan found it later and insisted that it be resubmitted.

This time Wight tried a London literary agent, who liked the book and sent it to the publisher Michael Joseph, ironically the house Wight had originally considered for the book but which a friend had talked him out of. Michael Joseph accepted the manuscript, which was published as *If Only They Could Talk* (1970). Wight was fifty-four years old. He felt he could not publish under his real name because the ethics of his profession precluded advertising, and he also thought that some of his colleagues would consider publishing a book about a veterinary practice to be unethical if he used his real name.

So Wight adopted the pseudonym "James Herriot," taking
the name of a soccer goalkeeper who was playing well for
Bristol City one day on television as Wight typed. To this day
almost all of his fan mail is addressed to Herriot, and many
writers ask if he is related to them or to a Herriot aunt or
uncle. He also changed the names of most of the people in the
narratives. What he may not have realized at the time is that
the changing of names allowed him leeway in his narratives to
shape and mold incidents and characters for creative purposes.
Wight claims that his tales are "90 percent true." But he also
has said that he is not at all "featured" in the narratives: "I
make myself as colourless as possible. I'm the Damon Runyon
character on Broadway, the guy who lives around." [13]

If Only They Could Talk was followed by It Shouldn't Happen
to a Vet in 1972. Both books were only moderately successful,
the first selling only 1,200 copies. Then a person came into
Wight's life who more than anyone except the author himself
created the figure of James Herriot, international best-selling
author. Thomas J. McCormack, president of St. Martin's Press
in New York, was on his yearly trip to London, visiting
publishers and agents in search of possible republications and
new writing talent. An agent handed him a paperback copy of
If Only They Could Talk. The agent was somewhat apologetic
about introducing a book on pre–World War II English
North Country veterinary medicine to a New York publisher.

McCormack took the book home, along with others, and
left it unopened in a pile on his bedside table. His wife,
Sandra, got to it first, read it, and one night said to him:
"You've got to look at this. If you don't publish it, I'll kill
you." [14] McCormack loved it, but felt it was not commercial
enough or complete as it stood. He obtained a copy of It
Shouldn't Happen to a Vet and was close to publishing both
books as one, but he still felt that the "book" was not complete. He communicated with Wight and asked him if he
would consider rounding out the story with a marriage.
Wight cordially complied, adding three chapters that, in

McCormack's words, "gave us . . . an ending that chimes as gloriously as *The Sound of Music.*"[15] He might have said "the sound of money," but thus *All Creatures Great and Small* (1972) was first published in America, where the Herriot memoirs still have their greatest popularity. The book jumped on the best-seller lists even before the reviews were in.[16]

Wight chose the title from the beautiful Anglican hymn "All Things Bright and Beautiful" by Mrs. Cecil Frances Alexander (1818–1895). Three subsequent Herriot titles came from the same verse, a favorite of children: *All Things Bright and Beautiful* (1974), *All Things Wise and Wonderful* (1977), and *The Lord God Made Them All* (1981).

Wight came to America in 1973 to promote *All Creatures Great and Small* and the next year to tour for *All Things Bright and Beautiful,* but after that Wight refused further promotional travel. Although he enjoyed the trips, he found it too difficult to return and readjust to veterinary practice, for he considered himself "99 percent veterinarian and one percent writer. The farmers wouldn't care if my name were George Bernard Shaw; they want their animals well cared for."[17]

While Wight was touring, two more collections of his memoirs were published by Michael Joseph: *Let Sleeping Vets Lie* (1973) and *Vet in Harness* (1974). St. Martin's combined them into *All Things Bright and Beautiful* (1974), and again Herriot was on the best-seller lists. American and British readers began to make pilgrimages to Thirsk to track down the unassuming veterinarian, basically a private person but always patiently willing to autograph books, to the extent that at this writing he suffers from arthritis in his right hand from inscribing thousands of books and has undergone surgery to relieve the pain. Now he signs his name to sheets of stickers to attach to books. It is easier on his hand. Ever the generous person, he still cannot say no to an autograph request. Many fans study maps of Yorkshire or consult travel books looking in vain for Herriot's town, "Darrowby," which is, in fact, a fictionalized composite of Thirsk, Richmond, Leyburn, Middleham,[18] and pieces of the here and there, as well as creative locations in Wight's imagination.

While serving in the veterinary practice, writing, and promoting the books, Wight was also elected president of the Yorkshire Veterinary Society for 1973–1974, and he also witnessed the first filming of his work: *All Creatures Great and Small*, shot in 1974 and released the following year, starred Anthony Hopkins as Siegfried, Simon Ward as Herriot, and Lisa Howard as Helen. The screenplay was written by the distinguished playwright, Hugh Whitmore. Wight went to watch them film in Farndale. He stood on the periphery of the shoot, enjoying seeing the old cars; meeting the celebrity actors; and seeing Simon Ward, who had just played Winston Churchill in a film, now recreating the earlier life and work of a country vet: Wight himself. On 4 February 1975 this film production was seen on America television in the NBC Hallmark Hall of Fame series.

Wight continued to work and to keep his diary and to consult it for further anecdotes and stories to incorporate in new books. Michael Joseph was happy to publish the initial shorter books that St. Martin's would later incorporate into longer books. Michael Joseph brought out *Vets Might Fly* in 1976 and *Vet in a Spin* in 1977, and St. Martin's combined them into the larger book titled *All Things Wise and Wonderful* (1977).

In 1978 BBC began to release its seemingly immortal *All Creatures Great and Small* series starring Robert Hardy as Siegfried, Christopher Timothy as James, Carol Drinkwater as Helen, and Peter Davison as Tristan. The series began showing in the United States on PBS the next year and is still being shown in reruns on various local PBS stations. Under the rubric of *All Creatures Great and Small*, the series used material from the first book through the events in *All Things Wise and Wonderful*. In the post–World War II episodes, Carol Drinkwater was replaced by Lynda Bellingham.

Another Herriot film, *All Things Bright and Beautiful,* alternately titled as *It Shouldn't Happen to a Vet,* starring John Alderton, Colin Blakely, and Lisa Harrow, was released in 1979 but not widely shown. In the same year St. Martin's included the text and photo book *James Herriot's Yorkshire* in their series of British authors and their regions. Wight provides the descriptions of and commentary on Yorkshire towns and landscapes in conjunction with the photos of Derry Brabbs. At this writing a film version of this text is in production with Christopher Timothy narrating and Wight appearing.

Wight's fame brought him honors and academic recognition in 1979, with an OBE conferred by Prince Charles and an honorary D.Litt. from Heriot-Watt University, Edinburgh. He was elected a fellow of the Royal College of Veterinary Science in 1982, and an honorary D.V.Sc. was awarded him by Liverpool University in 1983.

The fourth, and what was incorrectly assumed to be the final, collection of Herriot tales appeared in 1981 as *The Lord God Made Them All.* No Michael Joseph imprints preceded this American publication of St. Martin's. The American publisher was determined to keep the Herriot name in the public eye, publishing *The Best of James Herriot* in 1983 and *James Herriot's Dog Stories* in 1986. Additional recycling was achieved by having Wight take individual anecdotes or chapters from the early collections and turn them into texts for illustrated juvenile books such as *Moses the Kitten* (1984), *Only One Woof* (1985), *The Christmas Day Kitten* (1986), *Bonny's Big Day* (1987), *Blossom Comes Home* (1988), *The Market Square Dog* (1989), *Oscar, Cat-about-Town* (1990), *Smudge, the Little Lost Lamb* (1991), and *James Herriot's Treasury for Children* (1992).

Herriot thus has become a major author in the juvenile market with enormous sales and representation in almost all school and public libraries of the English-speaking world. The

implication is that this Herriot industry, created by astute
publishers, will be self-perpetuating at least for a generation
as the readers of the children's books grow into the readers of
the adult memoirs, viewers of the films and TV series extant
and surely forthcoming, and visitors to the living "theme
park" in the north of England, a region that could be called
Herriot country. The memoirs of James Herriot are a part of
the international tourism industry, geographical and literary.
Naturally there is a "James Herriot Yorkshire Calendar."

In 1992 Wight surprised and delighted his fans as well as
his publishers with yet another volume of memoirs, this time
with a title from the Old Testament, *Every Living Thing*. Some
600,000 copies were printed prior to publication date, and
the book immediately jumped on to the best-seller lists, re-
maining there for over thirty weeks.

Approaching his eightieth year, James Alfred Wight is a
happy and contented grandfather of three grandaughters and a
grandson. He has said that "Nothing important has ever happened to me. My life is merely the framework for a series of
animal incidents." [19] In fact he has translated his "life" into a
semimythic character that may have a continuing existence
and growth of its own like a Hamlet or a Hornblower.

It seems apparent that from an earlier stage in his career
as a veterinary surgeon, Wight has seen himself as an observer,
a chronicler, a midwife to what may be a unique animal-
care discourse that, like all discourses, is as revelatory of the
participants as it is about its subjects.

Recent visitors and interviewers of Wight responded to
him in the way that tens of millions of readers have responded
to the Herriot construct in the texts. They saw what is to
Americans the best of what it is to be "British": dignified,
secure in one's history and place, tolerant, fair, reserved, intelligent, modest, humanistically educated, loving the English
language, and projecting the empowerment of precise discourse. His hair was long and gray, his body was still compact
at the end of his life but less muscular than when he manhan-

dled cattle and horses. His face was round and ruddy and his eyes still very blue and twinkling with kindness, gentleness, and humor. His wide-palmed hands were those of a man who had worked skillfully with them all his life.

James Alfred Wight died of prostate cancer at his home in Thirlby on 23 February 1995. James Herriot lives on.

2

The Herriot Mystique

Old fashioned and romantic as it is, James Herriot's smashingly successful, long, professionally sculpted memoir in five parts succeeds with a wide general reading public because the author intuitively understands a dynamic of mental response —the power of reflection and re-reflection on certain elemental facets of life experienced, liminally, as *thought* by humans: the wonder and fierce determinism of birth; the fragility of life; the need for and power of community; the call of the conspecific within the mold of a rather Dickensian characterization; the primal appeal of anthropomorphism; the human commitment to the life force; the primate-originated deep pleasure of placing one's head and hand upon the warm flank of another mammal even if the action occurs vicariously in the mind; the sympathetic "magic" of healing; and the fearful inevitability and finality of death for all living things. Simultaneously, Herriot projects a seemingly ingenuous style in which his persona, gentle and self-effacing, a sensitive and boyish man, provides an inner narrative frame of imagination.

I refer to the Herriot saga as memoir, but it really is only partly so. It may be fruitless to categorize any narrative as exclusively fiction, or biography, or memoir, or autobiography, or history. Many "autobiographies" of novelists are indistinguishable from their best works of fiction and, indeed, have been written to forestall, divert, or trick later potential biographers. Herriot's tales are precisely constructed narratives, aided and shaped at least initially in early collections by or with editorial aid. He changes names in order to elaborate idiosyncratic characters as with the Farnons. He alters and mixes places with the result that, for example, Darrowby is a construct but York is not. Choice is the essence of art. The incidents Herriot selects from his experiences are carefully selected, reordered, and shaped for the strongest narrative impact. In other words, as a novelist does, Herriot draws on experience but frees himself, rightly, to divert and digress and to carefully align sympathies and antipathies.

Simultaneously, and most significantly, this freeing up of narration allows the reader to "free up" too. For example, Mrs. Pumphrey, if regarded as a "real person," who feeds delicacies to her overweight dog Tricky Woo and orders her old gardener to "nanny" the beast, would appear as slightly touched, more than merely eccentric, selfish, foolish, and in the Depression era, with children hungry in the community about her, something of a social criminal needing to be taken in hand and reeducated. As a fictive character she is a harmless, delightfully balmy, 1930s "Lady Bountiful." Thus, Herriot employs one of the oldest techniques of the homiletic storyteller, assuring us that his tale is true, when in fact it is a crafted remembrance or adaptation of experience, the primary function of which is not reconstructive but fictive, the literary magician's trick, a structured narrative built with an implied reader in mind.

On a superficial level, the Herriot memoirs are period-place studies of pre– and post–World War II Yorkshire, but in reality the author does not replicate a community; he creates one. Herriot's literary consciousness is more a sociohistorical one than a historical one; that is, it is not event oriented but community group oriented, although in *All Creatures Great and Small* the threat of World War II hangs overhead in the collective consciousness like the proverbial sword. Herriot crosses into discourse border zones where, surely disconcerting formalist readers and critics, he unself-consciously brews his individual recipe of memoir, fiction, social history, and veterinary science. The Yorkshire-Herriot world is more hierarchical than the actual Yorkshire of the 1930s. Herriot's lords and ladies, old family retainers, Anglican ministers, police, shopkeepers, wealthy farmers, subsistence farmers, and agricultural workers form a feudal construct much more reflective of eighteenth- or early nineteenth-century England, and although pre–World War II Yorkshire was certainly less politically and socially emancipated than places such as London, Liverpool, Birmingham, or Glasgow were then, still the social compacts of Herriot's world are archaic and simplified for the times depicted. James and Helen are solidly middle class with movement toward the upper reaches when, after receiving a partnership in the practice, having children, and completing military service, the postwar move to expensive independent housing signifies "arrival."

Siegfried clearly aspires to a gentrified lifestyle, with his specializing in treating horses of the hunter and racing varieties and his great pleasure in hobnobbing with gentry and the minor nobility, who conveniently dot the landscape of Herriotland. James's profession and association with Siegfried enable him to overcome both his outsider status and his marriage to a farmer's (albeit a fairly prosperous one) daughter, and allow him some association with the local establishment.

Forms of personal address receive interesting treatment in the books. James addresses very wealthy farmers and the gentry as Mr.; all women (except his wife of course) as Mrs. or Miss, implying strong comity and respect between men and women; poorer farmers often by their first names; agricultural workers almost always by first names or last names sans Mr. Yet one surmises that the audiences take little notice of this Toryism, and when and if they do they are not bothered by it, as indeed many of us have at least a dollop of need to dream of a simpler order and for a belief that a prelapsarian utopia once existed within the Great Chain of Being, with all strata of

Camelot happy in their place from lords, to burghers, to peas-
ant workers, and even itinerant gypsies. "All parts right and
functioning," Herriot might say. Popular literature is not
about Zolaesque realism.

The BBC TV series faithfully replicates the social structure of Herriotland. That effort is part of the success of the
ever-playing enterprise. Of course there exists, and will continue to exist for some time to come, an interplay and cross-
fertilization of audience of text, TV, film (now available on
home video), and, to a lesser extent, talking books and tapes
with Wight reading the text. Thus, the synergistic marketing
of Herriot is an excellent example of the efficacy of multimedia
exploitation to provide an introduction to a product via several
sources and multiple use. Packaging of a popular entertain-
ment product is a marketing art form. One suspects that today
more new readers come to Herriot from the TV production
than come to the TV production through the texts.

The hardbound St. Martin's editions, with their incremen-
tally aging jacket paintings of "Mr. Herriot" holding or loom-
ing over various assortments of animals, are collected by fans,
who see in the progressive publications and dust jackets an
airbrushed mirroring of their own maturation and aging. The
treasuring of the texts, their rereading, and the TV audience
that sees the series over again are all necessary parts of popular
culture iconolatry. I can recall that when living in York in the
1960s and listening to an early version of a talk show on the
Home Service, I heard listeners call in large numbers to tell of
their "epiphanic" experiences from seeing the film *The Sound
of Music*. What intrigued me was that so many reported paying
to view the new release a dozen or more times. That is cultish
power: the ability to retain a devoted interest with the financial manifestation of continuing revenue intake. Thirty years
later the synergies of pop marketing are much more refined
and effective.

Rereadings and reviewings of the Herriot texts and media
material provide for the massive urban and suburban postin-

dustrial consuming world the familiarity of conventional characters, bearing traditional morals and ethics, disguised as
eccentrics, and clothed in humor and pathos; vicarious partici-
pation in the socially desired but fantasied post–World War
II Norman Rockwell modernist victory of the tolerant over the
intolerant; much ease from difficult and problematic thought;
pastoral relaxation; a frisson from controlled vicarious association with a harder time and the harsher agricultural life of
almost all our ancestors; a simultaneous and paradoxical faith
construct of a benign nature of Wordsworthian proportions; a
companionship with our ancestral animal wards without the
actual stink and sight of feces and without the absurdity of a
description of just what it is like to live in a cow's body.

The five Herriot texts are essentially last-quarter twentieth-century tomes, and thus as mainstream popularist products, they are Green friendly. The moors and the mountains
are to be preserved. The landscape has a spirit and is loved.
Agricultural land is well tended over the centuries. Except for
the unfortunate fox, hunting and fishing are extremely rare.
People eat well but plainly and with little waste. The drink
of choice for men is nutritious beer and the occasional wee
tot of Scotch whiskey for the few who can afford it. The only
women who also imbibe an occasional beer are of the working
class. The human population is generally abstemious in sexual
matters, with marriages late and children few (two is the
nicest number for the middle class, one for the aristocrats)
with the exception of very poor (sometimes stated as Irish and
implied Roman Catholic), little-educated, and clearly unen-
lightened but well-meaning folk. The location is uncrowded.
The population is not rapidly expanding. In fact it seems
static. The message is conservation: conserve the ecological
balance of nature and humankind's needs. But the more sub-
textual message is conservative, physiocratic, strongly sup-
portive of the values of the dominant political culture: cherish
and preserve as much of human history and tradition as is
possible; do not let governmental folly destroy the natural

order of living things and especially society. (It must be noted that one character in the texts who becomes a governmental official is the flippant, self-serving, mostly incompetent imp: Tristan. Such an event implies, "Is that a way to run a country?")

Outsiders, although tolerated by the kindly local populace, seem to be rejected by the less-tolerant landscape. The gypsies move on, but the industrial worker turned farmer fails and must return to the production line. He carries a taint and a doom with him and is rejected by Mother Earth, for he is not one of her Yorkshire brood. The memoirs move up to and into the 1960s, but there is little reference to the new British, the Pakistani born and their British-born children of nearby Bradford and Leeds, for example. Did no one open a Chinese restaurant or an Indian curry palace in Darrowby-Thirsk? Did no person of color ever drive through, ever stop with a sick dog, cat, goat? Did no women or men lead alternative, visibly different sexual lives? Yet, despite omissions, the strong message of the texts is tolerance and acceptance of all life: human and animal. The pattern is opening not closing, inclusive not exclusive. If the great conflict of the twenty-first century is to be between the tolerant and the intolerant, Herriot is a politically and socially useful writer for the attitudinal development of the young.

Herriot is a healer-storyteller. Like a veterinarian in a local pub, the Drovers' Arms will do, he talks to his audience over a pint for the men, a sherry for the women, and a shandy for the children. He brings interesting characters on stage for certain scenes, removes them, and brings them back in another episode, flashing back and forth in time from the writing present to past incident, while all the time narrating within a framework of overall chronological advance. He speaks in simple sentences, deploying patterns of words to be heard. His prose is devoid of periphrasis.

A gentle narrator for polite and gentle people, Herriot paints late nineteenth-century "realism" with words: tense scenes of sick animals in stalls or cribs, near death; worried farmers (worried mostly about the economic loss facing them) with oil lamps in hand, bending over the perplexed healer who has been called from the arms of Morpheus and Helen, a healer desperately trying for a diagnosis and a cure with the relatively primitive curative tools available to him earlier in the century. We shall never tire of skillful tales of the drama of salvation and the mini-tragedies of heroic failure. Threading all the stories is the male human saga: Herriot the single outsider entering the territory of what is for him a closed tribe, finding acceptance through competent service, maturing, encouraged to wiving in young manhood, siring child, going off to fight for the tribe, returning alive to honor and full acceptance, and telling his tale to neighbor and stranger alike.

The Herriot prose mix contains humor, bathos, regionalism, "values" without distracting subtleties or contradictions, evocative description, an appeal to empathy, and a Deistic belief in the harmony of a God-created world functioning in good order, with only the fear that human-generated evil (such as war with the Nazis) could mar the natural perfection.

In her seminal work on popular literature, *Fiction and the Reading Public,* Q. D. Leavis says: "The reading capacity of various ages may be gauged by the demands made on each by its popular fiction, which since it was by definition widely read is the fairest test of the general reading level at any given time."[1] The great success of the Herriot narratives speaks fairly well of the reading public, much more so than if we are to evaluate the public's reading interest exclusively by the extremely popular romance genre, for example. The narratives are after all entertaining, moving, skillful essays written by a serious writer who served a long apprenticeship in his subject as well as in his craft. The Herriot persona has embraced the words of Marcus Aurelius: "Adapt yourself to the environment in which your lot has been cast, and show true love to the fellow mortals with which destiny has surrounded you."

3

All Creatures Great and Small

In *An Experiment in Criticism* C. S. Lewis points out that there is a particular kind of story that has a value in itself—a value independent of its embodiment in any literary work."[1] This kind of story perennially moves and appeals because it is archetypal; it is a part of the collective memory and experience of all humankind. We can never tire of its retelling, for the words of the story connect us with what is most basic within us: our need to love and be loved, our desire to care for those animals who have been brought within our dominion, and our hope that we and those who depend upon us will find, when needed, compassionate, wise, and skilled healers. *All Creatures Great and Small,* James Herriot's most famous and most successful memoir, succeeds in part because it combines three ancient narratives: the good herder saving his or her animals, the triumph of a healer, and the courtship of a young woman by a young man. We inherently know the ending of these mythic narratives. Our pleasure in rehearing lies in the cast of the retelling, for behind the suspense we know the requisite happy end. The myths of life—saving, healing, embracing— end in living, just as the myths of death end in dying.

Such is the appeal of *All Creatures Great and Small* that within one year after its publication in the United States by St. Martin's Press in 1972 it was a Book-of-the-Month Club selection and a *Better Homes and Gardens* Book Club selection;

condensations appeared in *Ladies Home Journal, Science Digest, Cosmopolitan,* and *Reader's Digest Condensed Books.* The Bantam paperback published in 1973 has gone through innumerable editions and millions of copies. New readers and fans of the TV series—three 90-minute specials and eighty-seven 50-minute episodes with additional material from later texts—in fifty-two countries[2] rise up perennially, like boundless fields of spring flowers.

Sometimes a book is so well titled that the appellation seems especially inspired. This surely is the case with *All Creatures Great and Small.* The line of iambic tetrameter, taken from Cecil Frances Alexander's hymn, is a pronouncement, a statement of the vastness and the unity of animal life, human and other. The line rings Biblical and echoes with the pure, innocent prelapsarian sound of a children's chorus. The word *creature* and the word *create* share a common etymological ancestor, the Latin word *creare,* to produce. Creation, God's and nature's, produces all creatures great and small indeed, and the creatures produce their kind and husband others. And of course, the storyteller creates too.

The 442-page book contains sixty-seven chapters, so the average chapter length is under seven pages. This fact suggests to me that the underlying, perhaps unconscious narrative structure of the book is the pub tale. In an agricultural area like rural Yorkshire the pub tale was and often still is about animals, with sports running second. Young Herriot, his employer Siegfried, and Siegfried's younger, ne'er-do-well brother, Tristan, certainly enjoy pub life, and the tale, at least in the days before TV and recorded music, was the chief accompaniment to the quaffing of multiple pints of beer. The tale needs to be short, certainly not lasting much longer than a pint, rich in characterization, splashed with irony or tinged with tragedy, and perhaps powdered with a dash of sex. The tale need not be totally accurate or truthful but merely seem so. Indeed some embellishment is expected. Chronology defers to subject and to the need for narrative effect. Herriot's tales flash back and forth between the author's present to his child-hood and training in Scotland, his arrival in Yorkshire, and events in his practice approximately during the years 1937 through 1939. Like pub tales, Herriot's memory-bits appear dialogical, and the effect that the narrator is talking directly to the individual "narratee" is part of the charm of the book. The modest Herriot narrator sutures the text through carry-over plots and through reappearing characters, both human and animal.

Speaking of narrator, it is probably best to discuss the intriguing question of who exactly is "James Herriot," veteri-nary and narrator? First, in general, memoirs are supposed to be autobiographical prose works located in the genre of nonfiction. The autobiographer is responsible for producing a series of events in some kind of sequential order so that despite flashbacks, splicings, and weavings, the narrative created ulti-mately takes the narratee from point A in a life to a point predetermined. Communication of truthful feelings and events is the assumed goal and is de rigueur. Unlike in fiction, where the author is not explicitly visible as the mediator, in autobiography or memoirs the author as narrator is assumed to be both subject and producer—totally and (sign)ificantly visible.

But I suggest that the author and narrator are not necessar-ily conterminous. In autobiographical writing the author as-sumes a certain persona either consciously or unconsciously. He or she may wish to hide facts or events, alter or amend others: distorting, airbrushing, refocusing, or spin-doctoring as suits the *construct* of the subject self he or she wishes to project and preserve as the "narrator." Professional biogra-phers are wary of autobiographies. They are often wrong in fact or date, human memory being fallible. At best, errors in autobiographical writing are accidental; at worst they are deceptions and even land mines to blow up biographers who may tread a road the biographee wishes closed.

Now what are we to make of a memoirist who uses a

pseudonym ostensibly to protect himself from being accused of using his writing as advertisement for his practice and who changes the name of almost all other characters in his work as well as place names? Is all this renaming done only to protect privacy? Is it not true that when this practice is commenced in the production of the text, a further degree of freedom from verisimilitude immediately becomes available as a writer's option? May an "autobiographical" author not be tempted to create a narrator to stand in for him or herself? Would this creation allow not only freedom from "fact" as best recollected, but also a defense against a possible charge of error, and, even more significantly, would it not also allow the possibility of further crafting of events, approaching the fictive, for the purposes of art, style, moralizing, symbolizing, and other purposes?

An interesting example of this tempting process is Siegfried Sassoon's autobiographical trilogy of novels: *The Complete Memoirs of George Sherston* (1937). In the three novels, *Memoirs of a Fox-Hunting Man, Memoirs of an Infantry Officer,* and *Sherston's Progress,* Sassoon relived and rewrote his own life from his Victorian childhood and his Edwardian youth through his traumatic frontline service in the trenches of World War I, but he did so as the persona George Sherston, slightly fictionalizing his own experiences. This fictionalization consisted almost entirely of two distinct actions: changing names of family, friends, and places; and, more significantly, eliminating his life as poet and homosexual from the memoirs. Thus, because everyone knew that Sherston "was" Sassoon, and that, seemingly in modesty, Sassoon was downplaying his great contribution as a combat poet by not alluding to it, Sassoon was able to conceal his homosexuality from the general public, heterosexuality being normatively assumed, and the lack of reference to any sexual life in the *Memoirs* was ascribed to decorum.[3]

In my mind the motivation for James Alfred Wight to "memoirize" himself as James Herriot was the opportunity for

greater artistic freedom. Wight is a creative writer. He is
a craftsperson who, in *All Creatures Great and Small* and in
subsequent texts, produced a unique panorama of pre–World
War II Yorkshire country life by means of an intricate personal
style in which characters, events, descriptions, the veterinarian's craft, and philosophical interpolations are interwoven to
produce an original tapestry. This several-stranded ropelike
patterning allowed the writers of the BBC TV series *All Creatures Great and Small,* despite the extension of subject matter
to later texts, to pluck select subepisodic segments and com-
bine them into a single TV episode. Typically, two to four
mini-incidents are spliced and interwoven for the hour pro-
gram, allowing the continual presence and development of
major and supporting characters and reintroduction of individual animals and specific locales.

Herriot, as Wight's carefully constructed persona, permits
the author to relate a somewhat idealized version of his own
earlier life in a character who himself is largely a sensitive
outsider-observer, a young city-bred man who is modest, diffident, lacking in confidence, and self-deprecatory, and who
comes to a fascinatingly different "another country," about
which in later life he develops a desire to report to the larger
world.

Certain of Wight's changes are clearly a part of his beautifully constructed Yorkshire "Nostalgia Land." The town of
Thirst becomes Darrowby, names of geographical areas are
invented, and the names of his subjects are altered to avoid
identification, although as far as regards his co-workers in the
veterinary practice, his wife, and his children, the name
changes in the text, slight or radical, offered little protection
of identity and privacy because Wight made little effort ever
to conceal his authorship of the Herriot memoirs. The name
changes permit, however, alternation of description, psychol-
ogy, actions, motivations, and events.

The most interesting alteration of names, accompanied
perhaps by the most interesting character and physical descrip-

tions, is Wight's change of the names of his employer, Donald Sinclair, and his employer's brother Brian, to Siegfried and
Tristan Farnon. Could Wight really have expected their true
identities to be kept private when, in part, he dedicated the
book to "Donald and Brian Sinclair, still my friends"? So
the question arises: Why the German first names? Early in the
text, chapter 2, Herriot ruminates: "Siegfried Farnon. Strange
name for a vet in the Yorkshire Dales."[4] He thinks that the
veterinarian he hopes to work for is a German who did his
training in the United Kingdom and stayed on, and who
Anglicized his surname, possibly from "Farrenen." Herriot
begins to imagine Siegfried in a not-quite-flattering Germanic
stereotype: "short, fat, roly-poly type with merry eyes and a
bubbling laugh" (AC, 9–10), which sounds a lot like Father
Christmas or Santa Claus.

While waiting for his future employer, Herriot encounters
one of Siegfried's girl friends, the beautiful, rich, debutante-
like Diana Brompton, who puts down and ignores Herriot,
thus damaging his fragile self-esteem and sense of manhood.
Later, while dozing in the peaceful Skeldale House garden,
waiting for the absentminded Siegfried to arrive for the hiring
interview, Herriot dreams about the absent "Herr Farrenen,"
whom he now dislikes for thinking so little of him as to miss
this all-important appointment and who has power over the
affections of a desirable woman who has just bashed his own
young and fragile ego.

In the light of sexual competition and a defeat, the new
construct of the "German" vet is less benign than the former.
In stage German, for Herriot loves to write in dialect, "Herr
Farrenen" spouts: " 'Wass is dis you haff dome?' he spluttered,
his fat jowls quivering with rage. 'You kom to my house under
false pretenses, you insult Fraulein Bromptom, you trink my
tea, you eat my food. Vat else you do, hein? Maybe you steal
my spoons. You talk about assistant but I vant no assistant. Is
best I telephone the police' " (AC, 17). Even in the dream,
Herriot recognizes that the accent is "corny" and, implicitly,

that the stereotype is absurd. Then he hears a "most English voice" saying "Hello, hello," and Herriot awakes to the sight of a tall, thin man, "the most English-looking man I had ever seen. Long, humorous, strong-jawed face. Small, clipped moustache, untidy, sandy hair" (*AC*, 17). So he is rescued from the German nightmare by an English hero named Siegfried, a man who, we later learn, has a womanizing brother ironically christened with the romantic name of Tristan. This burlesque scene is quite amusing, although out of keeping with Herriot's more subtle humor throughout the five memoirs. The description of Siegfried presented early in the memoirs is the only full one offered in the text. Little is made further of his physicality, and so the actor Robert Hardy in the BBC's *All Creatures Great and Small,* a very different physical type from Herriot's Siegfried, was able to go his own inimitable way with the character.

Four chapters later Siegfried says to James: "You must have wondered about my own queer name" (*AC*, 39). It is the reader, of course, who has been wondering. But the name is surely not a "queer" one. It is one of the best known in the world and a common enough German appellation. Siegfried and James both know its Wagnerian context. They subtly reveal that they are educated, cultured persons, and so does Wight. Herriot says: "I'm a bit partial [to Wagner] myself" (*AC*, 39).

Siegfried informs James that he was named by his father, a "Great Wagnerian. It nearly ruined my life. It was music all the time—mainly Wagner" (*AC*, 39). Donald and Brian Sinclair's father may have been a music lover or even a musician, but we do know that Wight's father was a professional musician. Wight's childhood was music all the time. His father lived through and probably participated in the great British craze for Wagner's music at the turn of the century.

Well what is happening here? What psychological reasons lay behind Wight's choice of the name Siegfried for Donald, and Tristan for Brian? Of course the obvious answer is that

Wight wishes to disguise his friends and professional colleagues, the Sinclairs. Furthermore, an English father who
names his sons Siegfried and Tristan might, to say the least,
be said to be a somewhat different individual. The author may
be trying to establish a family history of oddity to justify
building Siegfried into the charming, loveable eccentric he
indubitably is.

But it is early in the long memoirs, and the author reaches
initially for a burlesque German dream-persona, based on a
first name, to get a laugh. Perhaps it is an in-joke or friendly
dig at his colleague Donald. On the other hand, for an opera
lover to give a friend the pseudonym of Siegfried the hero is
also to honor that friend indeed. Yet there is a dark side to
the dream burlesque. Wight was born in 1916, during the
height of World War I. His earliest memories surely include
hearing post-Armistice anti-German talk. He served in the
RAF in World War II. Writing in the late 1950s and early
1960s, Wight allows the partially or totally repressed psychological construct of the Germanic stage, film, and political
cartoon image to emerge and then be expunged, erased from
the unconsciousness. Perhaps it was something Wight, the
British, and even the Americans of his and the next generation
needed to do. Done, the stereotyped "German" Siegfried disappears and the English eccentric takes over.

An author obviously needs to conjure a narratee to write
to. Wight has two constructs. The first is a general British
reader, a middle-class woman or man who loves animals, as
almost all British seem to do, especially dogs and horses. That
reader feels attached to the memory of ancestral work on the
precious land of a particular shire or riding, the centuries of
manor house and village.

Additionally, he or she anticipates, enjoys, and expects
"realism" in narratives. They must be "true to life." The
reader is secure enough, comfortable enough to read for delight and not as a part of an academic or self-improvement
exercise. The process is for pure pleasure, not for prestige or
profit.

Americans are also great animal lovers, and in our fantasies we often relate to the image of the glorified herdsmen of our past history, now known as cowboys, to the displaced American Indians who lived closest to natural fauna, and, of course, to the pioneer women who tamed the West, as well as the men who supposedly won it. Furthermore, no practical British or American author can neglect for long the fact that, numerically if not proportionately, Americans are the largest consumers of popular literary texts in English, and therefore the primary member of the first narratee construct must be English-speaking.

The author's second narratee construct is a practicing veterinarian whose life and work consists of caring for large and small animals and who, at the counter in the imaginary pub like the Drovers' Arms where the storytelling proceeds, could add his or her experiences with humans and other beasts to Herriot's, filling out the received texts with personal commentary, comprehension, and compassion. The narratee veterinary is presumed by the author to be interested in the near history of his or her profession, and so Herriot relates in great detail the procedures of the practice in the late 1930s, the era immediately before the seeming miracle drugs called antibiotics.

Veterinarian discourse, in fact, is one of the central architectonics of the text, and veterinarian terms for animal illnesses, medicines, and instruments provide chains of terminology that help to structure the work. The general reader is swept along the metaphoric route and either must understand professional discourse or let it flow over him or her like priestly incantations in an ancient unknown tongue. This largely unintelligible, arcane discourse of animal doctor–speak mystifies, bewilders, and simultaneously comforts—and all by design.

As if in a light rain, the reader is gently pelted with the details and accoutrement of "Veterinaria." Nostrums, folk medicine, arcane cures, instruments new and old, materia medica, and ancient and modern treatments parade through the text: linseed oil, bicarb and ginger, Epson salts, barbituates, electuaries, Jeyses' Fluid, manipulating impacted anal glands, cleansing the birth passage, a uterine valise, probangs (instrument for throat surgery), scalpels, directors (grooved instruments that direct knives), artery forceps, suture needles, probes, hypodermic syringes, epidural anesthetics, Nebutal (an anestheic), stripping udders, ung pini (ointment), Ziehl-Neelsen stain, tuberculin testing, Hexamine tablets, magnesium sulfate to precipitate insoluble lead sulfate, a Bagshaw hoist, auriscopes, pledgets, Chinosol, iodoform (antiseptic), ipecacuanha (produces vomiting), prontosil (early sulfon-amide), kaolin poultice, warm poultices, formalin (formalde-hyde solution), tincture of aconite, fleam instruments (for opening blood vessels), enema pumps, seaton needles, firing irons, blood sticks, sidebones (ossification of foot cartilage), quittor (purulent foot infection), and pulling the head of dis-placed femur over the rim of the acetabulum (hipbone socket).

Animal anatomy lessons include references to the rumen (first big stomach in a cow), the brachiocephalic muscle (arm and head), the mandibular salivary gland, maxillary (jaw) veins, the inguinal (groin) canal, the fascia (connective tissue sheath), the hock (hind leg joint), the withers (base of neck), the laminae (thin plates) of the foot, the stifle (joint between femur and tibia), the poll (nape), the jugular furrow, serum, and the epidural (lumbar area) space.

Besides attending to births and broken bones, James, Siegfried, and Tristan treat a compendium of animal illnesses including prolapse (falling) of the cervix, canker, aural hema-toma, pulpy kidney, retained meconium (feces that accumu-late during fetal life), nanberries (growths), papilloma (tumor) with a bibulous (spongy) surface, traumatic reticulitis (foreign body in the second stomach), anthrax, verrucose endocarditis (heart membrane inflammation), Johne's disease (enteritis characterized by persistent diarrhea), transverse presentation delivery, chronic mastitis (udder infection and thickening of the milk), eversion (turning inside out) of the uterus, retracted commissures (contacts) of the lips and a pronounced ascites (dropsy) as symptoms of an inoperable splenic (spleen) or hepatic (liver) carcinoma, erysipelas (infectious disease), milk fever, swine fever, lymphosarcoma, feline enteritis, acute laminitis (hoof inflammation), indurated (thickened and hardened) abscesses, and many other ailments that animal flesh is heir to.

The vets' discomfits range from the annoying to the dangerous: they must rise in the middle of the night and fight their ways to distant farms in all weather including blizzards, they are regularly kicked by angry beasts who do not appreciate puncturing, piercing, cutting, rectal or vaginal examination, dehorning, castration, or other indignities or intrusions. Enraged dogs bite the vets, frightened cats scratch them, and attack pigs savage them. Rumen gas knocks them over. And wild-eyed stallions mash them against stone walls or wooden stalls.

As mentioned earlier, another primary stylistic architectonic is the landscape imagery: the stark, variegated, sometimes intimidating but always beautiful vistas of Yorkshire seen through the eyes of the narrator, a city person who must either love or leave this unfamiliar environment of dales, fells, moors, and the Pennine Hills. The love comes early, like a powerful infatuation, and develops into a life-long, marriagelike commitment. Early in the memoir Herriot enjoys driving in "the high, unfenced roads with the wheeling curlews for company and the wind bringing the scents of flowers and trees up from the valley. And I could find other excuses to get out and sit on the crisp grass and look out over the airy roof of Yorkshire. It was like taking time out of life. Time to get things into perspective and assess my progress. Everything was so different that it confused me. This countryside after years of city streets, the sense of release from exams and study, the job with its daily challenge" (*AC,* 51).

Herriot is not only happy with his new country but also with the near environment of Skeldale House and Darrowby. Life was "the same every morning . . . there was always the feeling of surprise. When I stepped out into the sunshine and the scent of the flowers it was as though I was doing it for the first time. The clear air held a breath of the nearby moorland. . . . I never hurried over this part" (*AC,* 44).

Herriot's morning path takes him "along the narrow part between the ivy-covered wall and the long offshoot of the house where the wistaria climbed, pushing its tendrils and its withered blooms into the very rooms. Then past the rockery where the garden widened to the lawn, unkempt and lost-looking but lending coolness and softness to the weathered brick. Around its borders flowers blazed in untidy profusion, battling with a jungle of weeds" (*AC,* 44).

Finally, Herriot's memory walk brings him to "the rose garden, then an asparagus bed whose fleshy fingers had grown into tall fronds. Further on were strawberries and raspberries. Fruit trees were everywhere, their branches dangling low over the path. Peaches, pears, cherries and plums were trained against the south wall where they fought for a place with wild-growing rambler roses." (*AC,* 44).

The garden has long existed, surely planted a generation or more ago. It is an Eden with beauty and fruit, a microcosm of the Herriot world, a natural place of abundance, peace, and loveliness. The humming of bees competes with the song of blackbirds and the "cawing of the rooks high up in the elms." Life is rich, full, and satisfying for this young man, who is wise enough to accept the gift of a good world to live in, one that despite war and modernity will change little, allowing him daily to reflect in a Wordsworthian way that he is a tiny part of a vast, majestic, eternal landscape that has kindled his creativity and inspired his considerable descriptive power.

Three plot strands provide the great rope of the book: James the tyro learning of his profession with his concomitant acceptance in the town, in the dales, and on the fells; the battle saga of the brothers Farnon, Siegfried, and Tristan; and the courtship of Helen.

Fresh from veterinary school Herriot is understandably

unsure. An unexpected hurdle suddenly appears. Raised in the Glasgow area of Scotland, he cannot understand the Yorkshire dialect. Even before meeting Siegfried and obtaining the advertised assistant's job, Herriot meets his first linguistic obstacle, when the farmer Bert Sharpe appears at Skeldale House door to report that he has a cow "wot wants borin' out . . . she's nobbut going on three cylinders" (*AC,* 13). Herriot engages in a diagnostic conversation that totally baffles him: "I had listened to my first case history without understanding a word of it" (*AC,* 13). The dialectal barrier is soon overcome. Winning the confidence of the conservative, older Yorkshire farmers and horsebreeders takes longer and is more difficult.

Herriot's first solo case, after working under Siegfried's supervision, and undertaken when his employer had supposedly gone out of town to visit his mother (trips undertaken at odd times and hours implying a "Bunburying" escape to the fairer sex), is a very difficult one made more so by the arrogance and rudeness of Mr. Soames, Lord Hulton's farm manager. James has to destroy a prized horse and is threatened with a lawsuit and ruin if his diagnosis is proved wrong in the autopsy. Siegfried stands by him, cementing their relationship, and James's diagnosis proves correct. The case builds Siegfried's confidence in James, and James's confidence in himself. Later, poetic justice is served when the reader learns that Soames was corrupt, and having been caught and fired, comes into the surgery, hat in hand, to ask for help in finding a new position.

Gradually, the hard-working and competent young vet is accepted by the people of the region, but the road to acceptance is not always smooth, as when he diagnoses a broken pelvis for Mr. Handshaw's cow and condemns the beast to the tender mercy of Mallock the knacker for slaughter (advice that Mr. Hardshaw does not follow), only to learn later that the animal's pelvic ligaments had weakened temporarily after calving, and that she later regained her feet. Mr. Handshaw keeps the cow long after her normal working period just to show up a little the "young clever-pants" by displaying the animal everywhere with the speech: "There's the cow that Mr. Herriot said would never get up n'more!" (*AC*, 197).

The ultimate symbol of acceptance for young Herriot is the love of Helen Alderson of Heston Grange, a Yorkshire woman and a farmer's daughter. The courtship will be discussed further. Their marriage near the end of the book is the climax of the story.

The second plot strand, the fraternal conflict and sibling rivalry of Siegfried and Tristan, provides much of the delight and humor in *All Creatures Great and Small*. Siegfried, the older brother, has appointed himself father-surrogate; a senior Farnon, alive or deceased, is unmentioned in the text. But the great source of their guerrilla war is their radically different personalities. Siegfried is hard working, professionally committed, mercurial, short tempered, forgetful, generous when he is not worried about money, and inconsistent. He is genuinely worried over his younger brother's lack of success in veterinary college and Tristan's bon vivant lifestyle. Siegfried is infuriated by his brother's laziness, which is manifested in delightfully absurd ways as when Tristan is detailed to set the dining-room table: he bicycles between that room and the kitchen because the distance is just too far for him to walk.

Tristan is in no hurry to become a grown-up and accept mature responsibilities. He loves women, beer, sleep, and pub life, probably in that order. He is dedicated to rebellion against adulthood and his brother's controlling ways. This takes the form of practical jokes and doing as little work as he can. Siegfried is old beyond his true years, his late twenties, and Tristan is a Peter Pan determined not to abandon adolescence for as long as he is able to maintain it. He is Sir Toby Belch as youth.

The fraternal struggle begins with Tristan's return from school, after his having failed two of his course exams. Furious at just a partial disclosure of what has taken place, Siegfried throws Tristan out of the house. James is appalled at being caught in the middle of an internecine battle and then is shocked to find Tristan coolly accepting the fact that he has suddenly been relegated to the status of homeless person. Quickly, James learns that Siegfried's King Lear–like banishments of his younger brother have happened before and presumably will happen again, for the older brother's indignant rages soon subside, and his absentmindedness leads to the act of forgetting. Tristan is a master of passive aggression. When his brother gives him punishment jobs, he consciously or unconsciously fails miserably at them. Ordered to raise chickens for family eggs, and pigs for bacon and pork, Tristan somehow manages to let the pigs loose on an unsuspecting town, followed by Siegfried's mare, and the hens simply never lay for Tristan, although when given away they prove excellent producers.

However, beneath the fraternal conflict is genuine concern and love on the part of the older brother who is in fact parenting his younger sibling. And beneath the irreconcilable lifestyles and values differences of the two brothers, as well as Tristan's defensiveness, his denied need, his urge to perform crafty circumventions, and his passive aggression, Tristan has deep respect, admiration, and love for his brother.

The courtship-of-Helen, the third plot strand, begins with the meeting of the future lovers in chapter 40. James comes to her father's farm on a professional call to treat a lame calf. He is greeted by an attractive young woman in the farmhouse kitchen, and she escorts him to a field high on the fellside. Following the girl across a narrow bridge, he muses on the view: "this new fashion of women wearing slacks might be a bit revolutionary but there was a lot to be said for it" (*AC*, 245). James is moved to remark on the beauty of the place as, unbeknownst to himself, his heart has opened to the possibility of love: "The path led upward through the pine wood and here the sunshine was broken up into islands of brightness among the dark trunks, the sound of the river grew faint and we walked softly on a thick carpet of pine needles. It was cool in the wood and silent except when a bird call echoed through the trees" (*AC*, 245).

James mentions Helen to Siegfried, who tells his colleague that he knows and admires the "lovely girl." He informs James that she is popular: "half the young bloods in the district are chasing her but she doesn't seem to be going steady with any of them. Choosy sort, I think" (*AC*, 248). Helen desired by other males is naturally even more of a prize, and James's male ego is challenged. Also, the young man, far from his own family, who are never mentioned in the text, far from friends, and far from his Scottish home, is lonely. He is working desperately hard to learn his craft, to ingratiate himself with cautious, tightfisted farmers and difficult pet owners, to please his employer who has, unrealized by James, become a surrogate father to him—role model, advisor, caring provider, homegiver, teacher of an ancient art. Young women of the "right" education and class are few in rural Yorkshire, and the sight of the attractive and assured Helen, motherless, and assuming the women's traditional managerial and nurturing duties in the kitchen of her father's prosperous farm, poignantly appeals to the boy-man looking at a warm, comforting scene through the window of outsidership. Moreover, working in an economy that, after all, is almost totally reliant on sex, the breeding of animals for milk, flesh, hide, and wool, how could a healthy young man not be stirred? James's need for female companionship is palpable. Siegfried takes off to visit "mother" at odd times and hours. Tristan is a rake. James must choose the conventional way: courtship of a respectable young woman and marriage.

Comedy is part romance, the overcoming of obstacles in the way of young lovers, particularly the male in pursuit; and part satire, the indicating and indictment of human foibles, inappropriate manners, and sometimes vice. *All Creatures Great and Small* is a human comedy in which the overcoming is the winning of Helen that begins in the kitchen of a farmhouse and proceeds through a series of comic misadventures to comedy's inevitable goal, marriage, so that the human world may regenerate.

James joins the Darrowby Music Society in order to get to know Helen better, and while they are washing dishes together, he musters up enough courage to blurt out: "Can I see you sometime?" (*AC,* 276). Helen's face flushes as she replies: "If you like." The shy and bashful James has brought it off. The romance is on, begun during that most domestic of activities: washing up. A family is on its way to founding.

Yet "the course of true love never did run smooth." It really is not supposed to in comedy. And with Tristan as advisor what ever could go wrong does go wrong. For the first date the younger Farnon talks James into the pretentious act of taking Helen to a dinner dance at a posh hotel. He is to impress the farmer's daughter with his savoir faire, his generosity, and his too-tight tuxedo. His picking up Helen under the scrutiny of her father, and mightily amused younger brother and sister, provides the classic young male's first-date torture scene. Helen is stunningly beautiful in appearance "like a rare jewel in the rough setting of stone flags and whitewashed walls" (*AC,* 306).

Alas, things go wrong almost as soon as they leave the farm. The car runs into a flooded stretch, and the couple must push it through the water, getting feet and legs soaked in the process. Then they have to return to the farm so that James can borrow a pair of shoes from Mr. Alderson. At the hotel they learn that there was no dance that night. The meal is a strained and near silent affair, and when the couple shake hands to say good night, it seems as if James has struck out.

James is lovelorn. He is convinced that he has lost Helen's interest. He is sure he is doomed to life-long failure with the opposite sex. Later he will reveal why he is so insecure with women. On his first date at the age of fourteen, in Glasgow, a tram conductor caused him humiliation, and he never got over the embarrassment of the situation (*AC,* 402).

The young veterinarian of saintly patience is now ill tem-

pered. He hardly realizes it, but a torch for Helen is burning
in his heart. Of course readers are secure in their knowledge
of comic structure. The hero, they realize, must win the fair
maiden in the end. Meanwhile, however, Tristan's advice
causes trouble again. He convinces James that he will forget
Helen if he goes out with another young woman, and he
arranges a blind date for James with a nurse, who turns out to
be quite a pleasant and attractive person. Alas, James and the
young nurse cannot keep up with the alcohol consumption of
Tristan and his date. James and Nurse Connie get inebriated,
and, leaving a dance to get some sobering air, they fall down
a muddy bank and lie in the mud with their stomachs heav-
ing. Of course the worst happens: Helen and her date appear
at the dance and peruse the disheveled couple. James's rival,
the wealthy Richard Edmundson, who is mentioned only once
in this book but who makes several obnoxious appearances
in the TV series, peers disdainfully at his mud-splattered,
intoxicated competitor.

Thanks to Tristan again, James seems further away from
closing in on his heart's desire. Yet the reader is not sure
whether Helen is turned off by James's condition and company
or jealous that he is with another woman. The situation is
intriguingly ambiguous.

It is Helen, however, who makes the next move. She
brings her dog into the surgery with a dislocated hip, asks
specifically for James, and together they reset the joint. Later
Helen phones to inquire about the condition of her pet, and
James braves asking for a movie date. Helen accepts, and the
trembling swain realizes: "I was back in business" (AC, 392).
But the movie proves to be another risible situation for poor
James. He has expected that they would be seeing a film about
Scotland while cuddling in the "courting seats," a row of
old sofas. But James is immediately engaged by a customer's
complaining of the veterinarian's treatment of one of his animals. The romantic main feature is ruined for James by a
drunk snoring next to him. Then the expected Scottish film
with scenes of his homeland does not come on the screen.

Without an announcement the management has substituted a shoot-em-up, *Arizona Guns* (*AC,* 407). James is sure another social catastrophe has befallen him, but the wise Helen takes charge: " 'Look,' she said faintly, 'next time, why don't we just go for a walk?' "(*AC,* 408).

Now the paternalistic Siegfried, always trying to control the lives about him, butts in. He forces James to face up to the fact that he has been courting Helen. Then, to remind James, he presents a schedule of Helen's charms: "She is, from my own observation, extremely attractive—in fact she nearly causes a traffic pileup when she walks across the cobbles on market day. It's common knowledge that she is intelligent, equable and an excellent cook" (*AC,* 424). The setup closes with the rhetorical, "Perhaps you would agree with this?" Thus, he convinces his youthful employee that despite the fact that James is barely earning enough to support himself, he should "stop playing around and let us see a little action" (*AC,* 425). James, he argues, is too plodding, too apprehensive, and should be "plunging boldly ahead." His advice is, in other words, propose and marry. Siegfried simply assumes that Helen will accept, and he is right. The humor of the situation is that Siegfried himself is the most eligible bachelor of the three men, but he is not even vaguely contemplating marriage.

The impressionable youth now acts: he proposes. Helen says yes, and so Siegfried is responsible for James Herriot's becoming the father of a grown-up family while still a young man. Helen sends James to speak to her father. Interestingly, the author, with male reticence, gives far more space to James's meeting with Mr. Alderson to ask permission to marry Helen than he does to James's actual proposal. The two men drink a lot of whiskey and Mr. Alderson has to be helped to his bedroom. James, waiting for verbal parental consent, has to settle for a nod of the head. Yorkshire farmers are taciturn, and Herriot knows that "Everything most certainly was going to be all right" (*AC,* 434).

As Helen and James are about to wed, Siegfried commits

a typical reversal and now, because tuberculin testing time has come around and because the practice is overcommitted, he berates James for not looking ahead and "for belting straight on without a thought" (*AC,* 436). The ever-accommodating James volunteers to do the testing in a remote corner of high Yorkshire with Helen on their honeymoon, which turns out to be an idyllic experience and a wonderful way to commence a marriage of a veterinarian and a farmer's daughter.

The climax of this the most satisfying plot of *All Creatures Great and Small* is Siegfried's generous wedding gift to the couple: a new brass plate on the iron railing of Skeldale House, just below the one with Siegfried's, that reads, "J. Herriot M.R.C.V.S. Veterinary Surgeon," announcing that James is a partner in the practice and thus able to support Helen and the children to come.

Yorkshire's gift to the young outsider is a life of meaning in the loving fold of family and friends, and a place in the continuity of life. For the meaning of life in *All Creatures Great and Small* is simply stated: it is life itself, regeneration. The humans who live in the dales must regenerate too, for it is their own biological fate and their archetypal destiny as the caretakers of animal life. Herriot is not a conventionally religious person. For him, churches are for ceremony and for song. Religion is culture, but God, as in pantheism, is the life force.

Herriot is in love with life, the process and the experience. As a veterinarian he is at his happiest when birthing lambs. The vulnerable, soft, tender, meek infant animals stir his heart, for their coming in great numbers in the early spring is a sign of nature's covenant with both the protoplasm that knows and the protoplasm that transfers instinct. Herriot describes lambing joyously: "Lambs are usually born in twos or threes and some wonderful mix-ups occur; tangles of heads and legs all trying to be first out and it is the vet's job to sort them around and decide which leg belonged to which head. I revelled in this. . . . There are just two things to remember in lambing—cleanliness and gentleness" (*AC,* 147).

The great Herriot theme of *All Creatures Great and Small* and the subsequent memoirs is the assertion that humans are at their atavistic best when they exercise caring dominion over "every living thing." James, Siegfried, and Tristan are lovers of life. Helen and the housekeeper, Mrs. Hall, are nurturers. The veterinarians are Noahs husbanding animal life, keeping the herds viable, and safeguarding the livelihoods of ultimately all humans who live in the dales and on the fells. Even though slaughter for meat is the ultimate fate of the farm animals when either their working days are over or their fattening time has concluded, the veterinarians strive to keep the animals well in their allotted time, and they never take life easily. They not only fight disease but also suffering, and they deliver more mercy to the creatures than many humans find at the end of their lives.

Again and again James and Siegfried strive to stop the suffering of animals as, for example, when Lord Hulton's bay horse is in agony with a twisted bowel or when Mr. Dean's fourteen-year-old cross-bred labrador is dying of cancer. James informs the bewildered and trembling old man, who responds: "Then he's going to die?" Herriot swallows hard and offers: "We really can't just leave him to die, can we? He's in some distress now, but it will soon be an awful lot worse. Don't you think it would be kinder to put him to sleep? After all, he's had a good, long innings" (*AC,* 75). The cricket cliché rings somewhat false, as James admits, but he must keep under control his own pain over having to be the Angel of Death to a beloved pet.

When Ben, the dog of old, terminally ill Miss Stubbs, dies, and Miss Stubbs grieves that after her death she may not be united with her beloved animals again as she will with her parents and brothers, she asks James if he thinks animals have souls? James begs the question somewhat: "If having a soul means being able to feel love and loyalty and gratitude, then animals are better off than a lot of humans. You've nothing to worry about there" (*AC,* 270). She hopes he is right, and he offers a kind, white lie: "I know I'm right. . . . They teach us vets all about animals' souls" (*AC, 271*). The old woman reaches desperately for further assurance of his conviction, and he replies with a comforter's lie and, simultaneously, a great pantheistic truth: "I do believe it. . . . With all my heart I believe it" (*AC, 271*). In nature, indeed, humans and the animals they love and care for shall be together forever.

Siegfried's deep concern for and success in curing a little gypsy girl's suffering pony shows not only his great intuitive skill but also his deep compassion for animal life and, perhaps more significantly, his and James's respect for the "Other," in this case an itinerant gypsy family who, with their lifestyle and remoteness, precipitate suspicion in the dales (*AC, 379–86*).

Herriot also despises those who are cruel to their animals, whether out of greed, stupidity, arrogance, indifference, or insensitiveness, such as Farmer Sidlow who enjoys "God-like prestige" (*AC, 293*) but who murders his animals with "dedicated nursing," consisting of home remedies like "pushing half-a-pound of lard and raisins down the cow's throat three times a day . . . or maybe cut a bit off the end of the tail to let the bad out" (*AC, 293*). The Sidlows of agriculture lose their animals, but their cruelty cannot be undone.

The author, as a man writing in his early fifties in the 1960s about his twenties in the late 1930s, presents some interesting evolving historical attitudes toward gender and class. Women in *All Creatures Great and Small* are generally sorted into two categories: the workers and the rich. The former include farmers' wives and daughters who do the kitchen work, help manage the agribusiness, bear and raise the children, tend the gardens and the chickens, and, when needed, support husbands, sons, and male agricultural workers in the field and herdwork; housekeepers like the indomitable widow Mrs. Hall; nurses; and the bookkeeper Mrs. Harbottle. The rich women are threatening, emasculating, debutante types like Siegfried's friend Diana Brompton, who cuts poor James to the point of humiliation; eccentric wealthies like Mrs. Pumphrey; or ungrateful husband-father eaters like the spoiled Mrs. Taverner and her daughter, Julia, who bully and disdain the gentle millionaire, despite the fact that, or perhaps because, he has continually indulged their every whim.

The attractive Mrs. Taverner and Julia, a scaled-down version of her unpleasant mother, are more interested in faulting Mr. Taverner for their dog's condition than in showing concern for the rheumatic animal. The rich man is very poor in the quality of his life apparently because he has abrogated his manhood and has allowed himself to be ruled by women, thus causing misery for all. Taverner is lonely for sympathetic company, ostensibly male, and he is glad to have a drink with James when the hectoring women finally drive off. When James leaves the Taverner's palatial home, he sees the unhappy middle-aged man in the rearview mirror: "the figure at the top of the stairs looked small and alone till the high shrubbery hid him from my view" (*AC*, 395). The patriarchal message is clear: women indulged and uncorrected are a threat to masculinity, harmony, and family happiness.

Contrasting with the Taverners are the Rudds, small farmers, the author's favorite type of people. They have no car or telephone. Their seven children are healthy, polite, respectful to their hard-working parents, and generally well brought up. The Rudds are poor but generous. Whenever Herriot finishes a call, he is gifted with something from the meager larder, typically "a couple of home-made scones," and "three eggs" (*AC*, 335). All's right in this microcosmic world. Each denizen is happy because he knows his or her place, and Farmer Rudd can "embody the best qualities of the Dalesman; the indestructibility, the tough philosophy, the unthinking generosity and hospitality" (*AC*, 334).

The narrator invariably calls unmarried women of marriageable age "girls." Older women who are unmarried, like Miss Harbottle, are "Misses." Married women are always "Mrs." Helen is first a "girl" and then Mrs Herriot. However,

she is referred to as Helen Alderson, the full name, by Siegfried before she marries James.

Male bonding converges around beer and whiskey drinking. The pub is a male domain although women are sometimes
indulged in the parlor, and the drawer may be a barmaid. The
Drovers' Arms, a delightfully amusing name in its juxtaposition between its base cliental, the lowest rung of an agricultural society, the herdsman; and a coat of arms, the signifier
of the gentry and classes above. At the Drovers' Arms, men
can indulge in ritual comraderie and homosocial behavior in a
space taboo to the unsettling "other" sex. Drunkenness is not
frequent because the pub expects men to "hold their liquor"
and because local laws limit hours, although sometimes illegal
after-hours drinking occurs. Men must sometimes be bold.

Interestingly, the only time Siegfried is inebriated is when
he is off his home grounds at the Brawton races with VIPs and
hoping to obtain the choice position as supervising veterinary
surgeon for all meetings. He loses his opportunity because he
meets an old school chum and succumbs to the custom of
lubricating friendship with alcohol. After the amusing fiasco
Siegfried claims that he really did not want the job after all
because it would take him away from the beautiful hills he
and James love so much, but the claim reeks of sour grapes
(AC, 421).

Herriot the narrator is "unconsciously" class conscious in
a conventional manner, typical of Britons of his age and class
background. Agricultural workers are called by their first
names, although they address him as Mr. Herriot. Farm owners are "Misters" to Herriot. In respect to the upper class, the
narrator reflects the typical British middle-class ambivalence.
Nobility and old-money landed gentry, especially if they are
owners of fine horses, get all-stops respect, but the nouveau
riche, men and their wives or widows, such as the Taverners
or Mrs. Pumphrey, who have made their pile in the industrial
cities and come north to live somewhat like the old gentry,
are subject to a range of deprecation from good-natured, mild
satire to out-and-out scorn.

Class most decidedly wins out over money in the prestige wars. The deadbeat Major Bullivant, who has a Rolls Royce, is indulged because of his panache, style, and aristocratic chutzpah, and when finally this fiscal catastrophe for the community has to take his family and move on to greener pastures, he is missed: "Even after his departure Siegfried wasn't at all bitter, preferring to regard the Major as a unique phenomenon, a master of his chosen craft. 'After all . . . putting ethical considerations to the side, you must admit that anybody who can run up a bill of fifty pounds for shaves and haircuts at the Darrowby barber's shop must command a certain amount of respect' " (*AC,* 349). The American reader can certainly appreciate observing the skills of a consumate parasite, though he or she may be oblivious to the nuances of class attitudes in the author as manifested through his narrator. The reflected gender perspectives, however, are certainly current enough in both America and Britain.

Arguably, readers of *All Creatures Great and Small* find the near Dickensian characterization one of the most memorable aspect of the reading experience. Wight demonstrates great ability in limning colorful people who, although based on individuals he has known, are surely exaggerated for literary purposes such as satire and sentimentality. The international success of the BBC TV series is largely due to the fact that such broad-stroke characterization is dramatic, playable, and thus quite transferable to the film medium. Indeed the transfer would also be effective on the stage except for the obvious difficulties with the four-legged minor roles.

Siegfried, with his mutability and protean nature, is the keystone characterization. Tristan, like the "mercurial" god Hermes, is a jokester who likes to lead people astray. In Hermes's postclassical configuration he is called Hermes Trismegistus (the thrice great), and in an interesting echo Tristan is referred to or addressed with the diminutive "Tris." James is the stoic, tyro exemplar of Christian patience and ingenuous charm. He has near-saintly virtues such as integrity, loyalty, compassion, self-control, and truth telling (with a little white lying to spare feelings or avoid giving unnecessary psychological pain), but he is human enough to fall in love and to bumble about in courtship, to like a little drink, and to enjoy homey comforts as well as good company.

Helen is a perfect patriarchal, almost Victorian construct of "the good woman." She is virtuous, faithful, a good cook, a natural homemaker, and seemingly much more mature than her lover, although they seem near in age. She is the grand nurturer, the mother-wife, the dream woman: beautiful, intelligent, of good background, domestic, a co-worker when needed and deferential to her husband-to-be in the worldly sphere but expecting authority on the nest-building side of their relationship.

It is the supporting cast of characters who provide much of the richness and texture of the memoir. The first of the feature players is the delightfully dotty Mrs. Pumphrey, aided by her overfed, overindulged, but very goodnatured Pekingese, Tricky Woo. I can only smile while thinking and writing of them. The rich widow, based on the philanthropic Mrs. Marjorie Warner of Sowerby, who died in 1983, seems to have convinced herself that Tricky Woo, though acknowledged to be a dog after all, is her adopted child as well as "descended from a long line of Chinese emperors" (*AC*, 85). Tricky Woo, using the nom de plume of Mr. Utterbunkum (Herriot's signaled deconstruction of the fable) carries on a pen-pal correspondence via the editor of *Doggy World* with a lonely dalmation named Bonzo Fotheringham. Presumably, Mrs. Pumphrey takes dictation, but that is not stated.

Mrs. Pumphrey is James's great temptation. He loves the glass of sherry that greets him on professional visits and is quite willing to be Tricky's uncle James to ensure the continuance of Christmas hampers of delicacies and fine liquors from Fortnum and Mason. Mrs. Pumphrey is wealthy enough to create a world of believers in the humanity of the dog even as she overfeeds Tricky and endangers his life, which James must preserve by constant admonitions to his patroness and by removing the dog to Skeldale House for a low-calorie rest cure that includes running with the resident beasts. Mrs. Pumphrey acclaims the cure "a triumph of surgery!" (*AC,* 183).

The character who suffers most over Mrs. Pumphrey's indulgence of Tricky is her beleaguered gardener, Hodgkin, a dour old man whose conservative Yorkshire sensibilities are deeply offended by the indulging of a lapdog, and who hates having to exercise Tricky Woo but who, of course, needs his job in those Depression days. Things get worse for poor Hodgkin when his employer also adopts a pig named Nugent. The gardener cannot comprehend the name or handle the pronunciation, so, without any attempt at whimsy or satire, he calls the beast "nudist" (*AC,* 201).

Another significant feature player in *All Creatures Great and Small* is the older, heavy-drinking, mean-spirited, parsimonious veterinarian Angus Grier, "a cantankerous Aberdonian," who rather cruelly plays a practical joke on the neophyte James by having him wear a ridiculous "calving outfit," a rubber suit and hat, while performing postpartum cleansing of a cow (*AC,* 129). Later, when Grier has been injured, Siegfried sends James to Grier's place to take over the latter's practice while he is bedridden. Grier and his tightfisted wife treat Jim as if he were Nicholas Nickleby and they were the Squeers of Dotheboys Hall. Grier's treatments prove to be not only old-fashioned but inept, and when he has James use a folksy ineffective procedure, which must later be corrected by stitches, he perfidiously blames James for the bad treatment (*AC,* 208–9).

It turns out that the ugly, middle-aged veterinarian, whose skinny, anemic, pinched wife has a penchant for snooping, harbors a dark secret. A late-evening phone call from a Mrs. Mallard, whose dog supposedly has a bone caught in its throat, sends Grier, still incapacitated, into "a sort of trance" (*AC,* 210). Coming out of it he assures James, who must make the house call, that the dog merely has pharyngitis and

that some soothing medication is all he needs to take with
him. Arriving at Mrs. Mallard's, and expecting an old
women, he is greeted by a surprised "striking-looking blonde
woman of about forty with her hair piled high in glamorous
layers as was the fashion at that time. And I hadn't expected
the long ballroom dress in shimmering green, the enormous
swaying earrings, the heavily made up face" (AC, 211). Both
parties are embarrassed as James "treats" a perfectly well animal. Grier is an adulterer, and young, innocent James has had
a lesson in the facts of life.

The author is hard on the Griers and must have felt great
anger at the models for this couple, assuming this is a memoir
based on fact with only names changed. If so, Wight has had
his revenge, although in all likelihood the prototypes were
deceased by the time he portrayed the nastiest couple in all
the memoirs. One cannot help wondering, nevertheless, if
Grier, the improbable lover, called his inamorata, Mrs. Mallard, "Ducky."

The personification of death in Herriot's work has a jovial
face. Jeff Mallock is the knacker, the slaughterer for the
farmer's livestock, and the helper in all the autopsies to ascer-
tain cause of death. "In Darrowby the name Mallock had a
ring of doom" (AC, 165). The knacker's yard is the graveyard
of "farmers' ambitions" and of "veterinary surgeons' hopes."
His place was a vision of the apocalypse, requiring a strong
stomach to approach. The carcasses of dead beasts lay everywhere. The narrator evokes visions of catacomb burial with:
"Skulls and bones were piled to the roof in places and brown
mounds of meat meal stood in the corners" (AC, 165). But
Mallock is no gloomy, frightening, death's head undertaker.
He is pink faced, a "cherubic man in his forties, his wife
plump, smiling and comely" (AC, 165). His eight children
are beautiful and healthy even though they live their lives
surrounded by tuberculous lungs and a "vast spectrum of bacteria from Salmonella to Anthrax."

Mallock makes life difficult for the young vet, because he

continually confounds his diagnoses. Mallock has only four diagnoses for animal death and the most important is "Stagnation of t' lungs" (*AC*, 167).

Miss Harbottle, the secretary-bookkeeper, is another feature character whose appearances are threaded throughout the narrative. The narrator is very sexist in his description of her, and Siegfried is remarkably sexist in his treatment of the woman. Herriot describes her as "a big, high-bosomed woman with a round healthy face and gold-rimmed spectacles. A mass of curls, incongruous and very dark, peeped from under her hat; they looked as if they might be dyed and they didn't go with her severe clothes and brogue shoes. It occurred to me that we wouldn't have to worry about her rushing off to get married. It wasn't that she was ugly, but she had a jutting chin and an air of effortless command that would send any man running for his life" (*AC*, 90–91). So for the narrator, a middle-aged man reminiscing about his sexually insecure youth, Miss Harbottle's "problem" is that she is assertive, and that trait is sure to send men scurrying. The text assumes that she is unfortunate in not having had a chance to marry and that she did not have a chance at marriage. But that is an assumption, for she may have had proposals and declined. In a sexually clichéd manner the narrator assumes that a woman's life cannot be complete or be considered successful without marriage.

The fact that Miss Harbottle has had a significant thirty-year career with a big city firm in Bradford is apparently of little consequence to this somewhat immature male trio. Miss Harbottle is a strong woman in her fifties, and thus for the young men she automatically becomes a mother–authority figure. Siegfried reverts to childhood tactics to thwart the conscientious, hard-working woman in her attempts to do the very thing for which he has employed her; for although Siegfried refers to her as a secretary, Miss Harbottle is really an office manager who tries to bring order to his chaotic business. She cannot read their handwriting in the ledger, especially

Siegfried's, and she cannot believe that ready cash is stuffed in a pint pot on a mantle instead of secured in a cash box.

Herriot feels that Miss Harbottle "may be a demon of efficiency but isn't she a bit tough?" (AC, 92), implying that women must not be tough even if they are fifty and efficient. Siegfried, however, is quite sure he "can handle her." In fact, he mostly attempts to slink past her to avoid her criticism and demand for more professional business behavior on his part. For James, who never mentions his own parents in the text, Miss Harbottle is a "disapproving figure behind a desk" (AC, 104). Is she a psychological manifestation of a disapproving older female relative, or more likely one of Wight's early schoolteachers? The evidence may reside in Herriot's implication that Siegfried usually "looked like a schoolboy" when he faced Miss Harbottle (AC, 118). It is only by bluster that Siegfried is finally able to get the upper hand with Miss Harbottle, when he takes the offensive and mildly chastises her for not getting the bills out at the first of the month, when, in fact, she has been frustrated in her attempt to get him to input accounts so she can do the billing. By not listening and by controlling the conversation, he gets the last word, asking for "efficiency," but "Miss Harbottle's strong fingers close tightly round a heavy ebony ruler" (AC, 119). Is she the frightening but long-forgotten "school marm" after all?

Many of the characters whom the reader has come to know well in *All Creatures Great and Small* reappear in subsequent memoirs, providing a source of continuity for the magnum opus. For those readers who are "fans" of Herriot, these characters take on real human proportions and function as remembered friends or acquaintances with para-textual existences.

Lastly, the question is, What constitutes the ultimate subject of *All Creatures Great and Small*? It is not veterinary medicine as practiced in pre–World War II days. The true subject is Yorkshire, the beautiful, rugged, challenging country from the Pennines in the west, to the farm and grazing land in the dells and up into the high fells, and then across to the edge of the great North York moors. It is a place with great character, that changes little with time; a place where a young man from an industrial Scottish city could be captivated by a natural beauty never fully tamed by centuries of human labor; a place where any visitors today, and in the years to come, may roam about and believe that they are in Herriotland, and it would be quite true. There, as in *All Creatures Great and Small,* the air of goodness is breathable.

Of myth and reality, of fact and of fiction, *All Creatures Great and Small* belongs to that especially satisfying subgenre of literature, the *Bildungsroman.* The reader of the text and the viewer of the TV series take collaborative pleasure in the process of reifying a middle-aged man's happy remembrance of a youthful time of love, male bonding, growth, awakening, service, espial, and self-discovery.

4

All Things Bright and Beautiful

It is good to be reminded from time to time how satisfying an ordinary life can be—perhaps even our own. Alf Wight continues to do this in—*All Things Bright and Beautiful,* and as of 1992 an appreciative reading public had bought some four million copies, just as it had gorged itself on its predecessor *All Creatures Great and Small* to the tune of ten million hardcover and paperback copies worldwide. [1]

All Things Bright and Beautiful is, happily, a more of the same, please-do-feel-good-book. Without a hint of cynicism, the author had hit on an excellent formula, a perfect mixture of nostalgia, characters, old-fashioned personal and community values, interesting locale, and many loveable animals, poured into forty-eight draughts in a 378-page book. Wisely, the author decided to run his young life by us one more time and so rummaged through his experience and imagination to back and fill the re-creation of his early life from his arrival in Yorkshire as a twenty-three-year-old neophyte veterinarian to his departure for wartime service with the RAF, almost four years later. The incidents and related brief tales in this sequel are at least the equal of those in its predecessor, proving that the author's first work was not a one-shot inspired phenomenon but, rather, that he is indeed a consumately skilled storyteller.

In *All Things Bright and Beautiful,* the narrator Herriot

chooses to reflect on the domestic pleasures of a youthful marriage and the remembered triumph of a successful courtship. The memoir of a happily married man, dedicated to his wife, rightly commences in bed. The opening sentence: "As I crawled into bed and put my arm around Helen it occurred to me, not for the first time, that there are few pleasures in this world to compare with snuggling up to a nice woman when you are half-frozen." [2]

Herriot is soon called out from his pleasure by an inebriated farmer with a ewe in trouble. To reach and save the animal and her lambs, he endures freezing cold, gale force winds, and, worst of all for a man who loves music and plays piano, the raucous singing of the farmer, who keeps James in the cold while he slowly dresses. Afterward, James must wash in the field with icy water. Still the episode ends happily and humorously, for although Herriot will soon be asleep again in his connubial bed, Farmer Ingledew's neighbors must continue to endure the caterwauling.

The central binary of the total text is located in this first story: the contrast and relationship between Herriot's personal life with Helen, Siegfried, and Tristan, and his professional life with the client farmers and petowners and with their suffering animals.

In chapter 2 Herriot establishes the parameters of the text. He commences the retrospective around the time immediately after Helen's and his "unorthodox tuberculin testing honeymoon" and the setting up of their first home by making a one-room apartment of the spartan, waterless, third floor of Skeldale House, and he eventually ends with his call up for military service in the RAF for which both he and Siegfried have volunteered. In fact, the text wanders farther afield, back to Herriot's bachelor days with the Farnon brothers and to his courtship of Helen, which he now elaborates on. Herriot also emphatically states that he is not going to write about the war here. Events far away from Darrowby are inadmissible to the narrative (*ATBB*, 10).

Chapter 2 opens with Herriot back in bed where he can easily gaze upon his two loves: Helen and the Yorkshire landscape.

> I had only to sit up in bed to look right across Darrowby to the hills beyond. I got up and walked to the window. It was going to be a fine morning and the early sun glanced over the weathered reds and greys of the jumbled roofs, some of them sagging under their burden of ancient tiles, and brightened the tufts of green where trees pushed upwards from the gardens among the bristle of chimney pots. And behind everything the calm bulk of the fells. It was my good fortune that this was the first thing I saw every morning; after Helen, of course, which was better still. (*ATBB*, 10).

This chapter introduces one of the two main subjects in *All Things Bright and Beautiful:* the loving relationship between Helen and James presented as a recollection, from the perspective of 1970, of their difficult time in the late Depression and in the early days of World War II. Like any young couple Helen and James must define their respective gender roles. James tries to assert his manly right of protective self-sacrifice by insisting that Helen give him the uncomfortable, too-short chair to sit on as they try to eat at the bench they use for a table. She refuses. He speaks severely: "Get off that chair!" (*ATBB*, 11) but to no avail. James considers pulling her from her chair, but Helen is a big woman, and James is not a particularly large man. In previous good-natured tussles she has held her own, and James decides not to try the issue by force. He sits on the stool.

Herriot makes the point that although Helen is a traditional woman, who will cook, keep house, and bear their children, she will not be bullied, and she will insist on her primacy in the conventional distaff areas. Who sits where, and on what, when dining is within the wife's domain. Another

more successful veterinarian, out of an enormous generosity, manipulates Herriot into overeating and inebriation. James is simply unable to say no to his importuning senior, but it is also clear that he enjoys the drink very, very much . . . again and again despite wretched stomach illness and dangerous drives home.

Another humorous incident revolves around alcohol. Farmer Crump is proud of his homemade wines, and he offers James a sample. Herriot has not eaten dinner yet, and so he modestly requests an "aperitif." Mr. Crump brings out his "rhubarb," and then in succession his "elderflower, black-berry, parsnip and dandelion, cowslip and parsley, clover, gooseberry, beetroot and crab apple," and "incredibly . . . some stuff made from turnips" (*ATBB*, 62). Loaded, James must drive at a walking pace to an emergency call. The farmers there, it later turns out, are Methodist teetotalers, and we never quite know what they think of the intoxicated vet, who nevertheless does get his job done successfully.

As Siegfried is about to go off to the war, he and James have "a farewell drink" of whisky by the fireplace, and Siegfried shows his great generosity by informing James that he has found that he owes him fifty pounds for past work. Although James does not realize it at the time, the money is a gift to help him and Helen get by when James is also in the service. It is a sentimental time, for the friends do not know if they will ever see each other again, and they stay up talking and presumably drinking until 5:00 A.M., something they have done before (*ATBB*, 330–31).

Tristan's drinking and frequent inebriation complements James and Siegfried's imbibing. It is possible that the author may be both encoding and denying a problem with alcohol shared with his pals, a problem that perhaps results from the homosociality of the pub, which is the chief place of recreation for the men of a somewhat sexually segregated community.

.   .   .

In spinning his extended tale of the early years of his marriage in *All Things Bright and Beautiful,* Herriot revisits courting days, reveling over his delicious victory over rival, Richard Edmundson, who was introduced in *All Creatures Great and Small.* In fact, Herriot gives Edmundson much more attention in *All Things Bright and Beautiful.* Early on, Tristan informs James that the Edmundsons are old friends of Helen's family, "big farmers, rolling in brass. I understand old man Alderson fancies Richard strongly as a son-in-law" (*ATBB,* 50). Later, at the Darrowby Show, James is disconcerted by the sight of Helen with Edmundson (*ATBB,* 90), and he is depressed when, about to drive off in his battered little Austin, he sees Helen and Edmundson in the "front seat of a gleaming, silver Daimler" with the two fathers in the back seat (*ATBB,* 98).

Herriot's romantic triumph is the climax of the courtship sequences of the marriage plot of the text. At a dance he sees Helen dancing with "the inevitable Richard Edmundson, his shining gold head floating above the company like an emblem of doom" (*ATBB,* 280). James feels that his suit is doomed and his world is empty, but victory is snatched from the jaws of defeat when a client calls him away from the dance. The nearby Helen touches James' hand as he, hopelessly unable to speak in the presence of "her dark beauty," is about to leave. In a moment of courage he will never forget he says: "Come with me" (*ATBB,* 281). She does. They go to Skeldale House to get his instruments, and they begin a round of kissing from hallway to dispensary, and finally among the fragrant flowers in the garden (*ATBB,* 281–82). The call is to deliver pups, and Helen helps. Symbolically, their relationship is fixed over the process of helping life into the world. As the chapter ends, the dog's mistress says: "I suppose this is your young lady? (*ATBB,* 286). James puts his arm around Helen's shoulders and says "Yes . . . this is my young lady" (*ATBB,* 286). Thus, an unexpected romantic triumph can remain in the foreground of a man's thoughts throughout his subsequent lifetime.

The climax of the Helen-James relationship strand is the announcement of Helen's pregnancy, which comes, somewhat oddly, in a chapter almost entirely devoted to the farewell all-night drinking party of the friends Siegfried and James (*ATBB,* 328). But more significant is that without planning to, the young couple are contributing to the life of Yorkshire, ironically just as thousands of mothers' sons are going off to wounds or death. The dénouement of the marriage plot is Helen's tearful farewell to James as he departs to war, a scene that as portrayed in the TV series proves to be about the most moving of all the episodes. "Helen was in the window. She was crying. When she saw me she waved gaily and smiled, but it was a twisted smile as the tears flowed" (*ATBB,* 378). Herriot swallows the lump in his throat and vows that "nothing, nothing, nothing would ever get me away from her again" (*ATBB,* 378).

All Things Bright and Beautiful is a touching story of married love lived and remembered. The text's second subject is Yorkshire, with its flora and fauna lovingly portrayed once more as in *All Creatures Great and Small.* Herriot loves the high country and is always reluctant to come down from it. When he should be driving back to the surgery, he finds that the "old Drovers' Road" beckons irresistably: The "broad green path wound beguilingly over the moor top between its crumbling walls and almost before I knew, I was out of the car and treading the wiry grass" (*ATBB,* 40).

From the hill's edge he gazes down on Darrowby and feels the wind as "only a whisper and the spring sunshine hot on my face. The best kind of sunshine—not heavy or cloying but clear and bright and clean as you find it down behind a wall in Yorkshire with the wind singing over the top" (*ATBB,* 40). He luxuriates in visual delight and in the sensation of warmth from the sun. The break from work and routine to commune with nature is important to Herriot's well-being: "This form of self-indulgence had become part of my life and still is" (*ATBB,* 40).

Herriot devotes two chapters to a description of a "country show" similar to an American county agricultural fair. Animals are shown and judged. Riding-horses from children's ponies to huge hunting horses gallop in rings while "judges hovered around a group of mares and their beautiful little foals" (*ATBB,* 81). The bandsmen aged fourteen to seventy play on, doffing "their uniform tunics as they sweated in the hot sun" (*ATBB,* 81). Herriot enjoys recollecting the sights, smells, and sounds of simple country outings in the halcyon days before World War II.

A sheepdog trial is also lovingly described, the dogs happy and eager to compete. Always at his stylistic best in scene setting, Herriot takes us from the car park through the entrance gate, where

> The field was on the river's edge and through a fringe of trees the afternoon sunshine glinted on the tumbling water of the shallows and turned the long beach of bleached stones to a dazzling white. Groups of men, mainly competitors, stood around chatting as they watched. They were quiet, easy, bronzed men and as they seemed to be drawn from all social strata from prosperous farmers to working men their garb was varied; cloth caps, trilbies, deerstalkers or no hat at all [Wight almost never wears a hat]; tweed jackets, stiff best suits, open necked shirts, fancy ties, sometimes neither collar nor tie. Nearly all of them leaned on long crooks with the handles fashioned from ram's horns" (*ATBB,* 275).

Christmas in Yorkshire is charged with "the air of subdued excitement which started days before with folks shouting good wishes and coloured lights winking on the lonely fellsides and the farmers' wives plucking the fat geese, the feathers piled deep around their feet. And for fully two weeks you hear the children piping carols on the street then knocking on the door for sixpences, And best of all, last night the methodist choir had sung out there, filling the night air with rich, thrilling harmony" (*ATBB,* 171). This Dickensian passage is indicative of the author's growing skills as a descriptive writer.

Veterinary terminology and pharmacopoeia form an architectonic in this text too. Herriot talks his art and cites his tools, techniques, and medicines. As he discourses with the relatively few veterinarian readers, his writer's eye is really on us, and he impresses us with his professional parlance: blackleg vaccine, catechu (astringent), drenching bottle, stilbestrol (estrogenic), kaolin (absorbent), chlorodyne mixture (narcotic), decoction of hematoxylin (stain), infusion of caryophyllin (flavoring), Pituitrin (to induce parturition), agglutination tests, creosote (antiseptic), thiopentone (British variant of thiopental, an anesthetic), diethylcarbamazine (ureal compound), arecoline, morphine hydrochloride (sedative), carbolic (phenol disinfectant), pulvaromat (flavoring for medicine), bloodless castrations, turpentine, chloroform, arsenical expectorants, tincture of camphor, sodium salicylate, opium, bismuth, E coli antiserum, acriflavine (antiseptic) pessaries, *Black's Veterinary Dictionary,* and neomycin.

Herriot describes diseases, operations, animal injuries, and hazards to beasts: faecalith, acetonemia (slow fever—acid in blood), symphyseal (fused bones) fractures, tumefactions, coccidiosis (fungus disease), fistulous (ulcerous) withers, intussusception (intestine inversion), brucellosis (bacterial infection), colic (belly pains), decayed cotyledon (villi patches), clostridium (anaerobic bacteria), derangements of the parathyroid, salmonella, pulpy kidney, grass staggers: hypomagnesemia (caused by lack of magnesium), edema, lymphangitis, hysterectomy, husk (parasite-caused bronchitis), emphysema, pneumonia, pleurisy, copper deficiency, testicle tumors, entropion, sertoli cell (by testis) tumor, gastroenteritis, contagious bovine abortion, glanders (equine lung infection), strangles (throat swelling), white scour (bacterial enteritis), and tetanus.

The animal anatomy lesson continues: metacarpals (between wrist and fingers), ulna (inner forearm bone), radius (forearm bone), phalanges (digital bones), perineum (region between rectum and genitals), anconeus (elbow muscle), epicondyles (head of humerus), pastern (horse's foot between fetlock and hoof), lumen (inner passage of tubular organ), hock, and cartilaginous rings in the trachea. No wonder that when Herriot goes off to war, he packs his copy of *Black's Veterinary Dictionary* out of fear that he might forget all that he has worked so hard to learn (*ATBB,* 377). Yet despite all the knowledge to be acquired, "the difficult thing about being a country vet is that first you have to catch your patient."[3]

The clinical climax of *All Things Bright and Beautiful* occurs in most dramatic form near the end of the memoir. Farmer Clark's calves are dying of white scour and Herriot's pharmacopoeia cannot help them. Knacker Mallock, the easygoing Angel of Animal Death, arrives to take his toll, but James wants to try new medicine that has just been developed, sulfapyridine, one of the sulfonamides, the first true antibiotics, discovered immediately before World War II, and true killers of disease-causing bacteria. Mallock is patient, and Farmer Clark allows James to administer the tablets that arrived that very morning. The age of miracle medicine arrives for the animals of Yorkshire when the calves are cured overnight. James is thrilled to have witnessed the medical revolution of the twentieth century, but Mallock's accolade is predictable: "Them little blue tablets must have good stuff in 'em. They're fust things I've ever seen could cure stagnation of t'lungs" (*ATBB,* 358).

"My books are a restatement of old values: hard work and integrity. You can see them on the farms here in Yorkshire all the time and it's quite a contrast to what one finds in city life today" said James Alfred Wight in a 1986 interview.[4] Sexual immorality hardly appears in Herriot's Yorkshire, with Angus Grier's pathetic and risible affair in *All Creatures Great and Small* the sole exception. Sex between humans is little discussed in *All Things Bright and Beautiful* or elsewhere in the

Herriot canon, although the product of sex—children—have an important place in the oeuvre. James is always anxious at night to get back in bed with the beautiful Helen, but it appears that his main desire is to get warm. Even animal sexual activity receives little direct attention except for the function of bulls, although the provincial community exists on the reproduction of animals. And there is the paradox: sex has to be something of a bore to people who see it performed all the time in the barnyard, the field, and at the kitchen door by the chickens. It is a sloppy, violent, funny, necessary business and seems to have little to do with love and affection.

Lust is a male thing and rather bestial. Herriot seems to be both laughing and allegorizing when he describes the obsessive but futile passion of male dogs, ironically for a poor male dog suffering from a disease that has upset his hormone production:

> Percy was under siege, and as the word got around the pack increased, being augmented by several of the nearby farm dogs, a Great Dane who had made the journey from Houlton, and Magnus, the little dachshund from the Drovers' Arms. The queue started forming almost at first light and by ten o'clock there would be a milling throng almost blocking the street. Apart from the regulars the odd canine visitor passing through would join the company, and no matter what his breed or size he was readily accepted into the club, adding more to the assortment of stupid expressions, lolling tongues and waving tails; because, motley crew though they were, they were all happily united in the roisterous bawdy camaraderie of lust"(*ATBB*, 220–21).

Now is this Herriot's satiric comment on male bonding? Accidental or not, the implied connection to the "boys" at the bar of the Drovers' Arms is delightful to contemplate.

But food is something to get turned on about. Food is the farmers' lust. Except for a small number of men addicted to drink, eating is the supreme pleasure, the "consuming passion," especially for men and women who do so much hard physical work and for whom, more often than not, money is short and purchased victuals hard to come by. Herriot enjoys depicting meals and recording the "menus." When, during the courtship, James is invited by Helen to her home for a Sunday Yorkshire "tea," the repast has been created by the young woman perhaps in audition for the role of conventional wife. The board groaned with the weight of the food: "I was relieved when Helen came in carrying a cake which she placed on the big table. This wasn't easy as the table was already loaded; ham and egg pies rubbing shoulders with snowy scones, a pickled tongue cheek by jowl with a bowl of mixed salad, luscious looking custard tarts jockeying for position with sausage rolls, tomato sandwiches, fairy cakes. In a clearing near the centre a vast trifle reared its cream-topped head. It was a real Yorkshire tea" (*ATBB,* 52).

Herriot describes a lunch provided by a colleague's wife: "something with the unassuming name of fish pie but in truth a magical concoction in which the humble haddock was elevated to unimagined heights by the admixture of potatoes, tomatoes, eggs, macaroni and things only Ginny knew. Then the apple crumble and the chair close to the fire with the heat from the flames beating on my face" (*ATBB,* 182). Of course it is women who provide for male pleasure, via food if he prefers, or sex when he is so inclined.

As in *All Creatures Great and Small,* the main source of reader contentment is the author's ability to create fascinating characters, some of whom are continued from the first memoir. Joe Mulligan and his monster dog Clancy are present again and Clancy is still "womitin' " (*ATBB,* 27). Of course Siegfried continues in his contradictory ways. Tristan remains the loveable scamp with "the Gods . . . looking after him as usual. In fact, I think the Gods love people like Tristan who sway effortlessly before the winds of fate and spring back with a smile, looking on life always with blithe optimism" (*ATBB*, 346). Perhaps his best "rag" is his portrayal of the cowled ghost of a fourteenth-century monk murdered at nearby Raynes Abbey. Tristan haunts the ruins at night until a burly policemen chases him into a wet drain pipe. Tristan suffers in the end of course, but the prank is memorable (*ATBB*, 137). However, he is maturing, having qualified at last as a veterinarian, and preparing to take over the practice when James leaves for service.

New characters enrich the text. The portrait of Mr. Pickersgill is a classic study in malapropism worthy of any eighteenth-century comedy or of a Dickens character. If a little learning is not always a dangerous thing, it is often a funny thing. Farmer Pickersgill, a good stocksman with a small herd, once attended a two-week course of instruction for agricultural workers at Yorkshire's Leeds University. "This brief glimpse of the academic life had left an indelible impression on his mind. . . . No capped and gowned don ever looked back to his years among the spires of Oxford with more nostalgia than did Mr. Pickersgill to his fortnight at Leeds" (*ATBB*, 33).

Pickersgill's vocabulary has slipped since his long ago "college days." He phones Herriot from the "cossack" in the village to treat a calf for "semolina," meaning salmonella. The animal is bleeding from the "rectrum," and the farmer wants a feces sample sent to the "labrador," although he is convinced that the calf's problem is due to the fact that the animal bled at birth from its "biblical" cord. Pickersgill does not want to be charged an "absorbent" price and he knows from experience that troubles come in "cyclones" (*ATBB*, 38–39).

Mrs. Dalby epitomizes Herriot's Victorian "Good Woman," Yorkshire farmer variety. Her strong husband dies of early cancer, leaving her with a small farm on marginal land and three young children. "The general opinion was that Mrs. Dalby should sell up and get out. . . . It was a poor place and a woman would never make a go of it" (*ATBB*, 99). Calamity strikes, and her herd falls deathly ill, partly because of her inexperience, and the compassionate Herriot is heartbroken over her fate. But she endures a second near disaster and perserveres. Her sons grow into hardy manhood. She never remarries, but keeps a shrinelike photo of her deceased husband on the mantlepiece, and she continues to mark her wedding anniversary twenty years after widowhood. Mrs. Dalby never complains, never is angry at her hard fate, and never regrets "the years of struggle, the nights of worry and tears, the grinding toil" (*ATBB,* 115). She is almost too good to be true. Of course she always has delicious food ready for Herriot when he makes a professional call. Her last words in the text are: "Mr. Herriot, are you quite sure that tea is to your liking?" (*ATBB,* 115).

Old Mrs. Donovan, a busybody, is one of several characters in the Herriot canon who are amateur vets and who second-guess Herriot, frequently providing his cliental with free advice and nostrums of dubious value. She seems "ageless" to Herriot, probably because she is postmenopausal and thus of little physical interest to some men: "she seems to have been around a long time but she could have been anything between fifty five and seventy five" (*ATBB,* 70). When her pet terrier is killed James arranges for her to care for a cruelly mistreated young Golden Retriever, and the animal thrives. She is a superb pet owner, and Herriot's praise of her caring skills makes her his friend. As the years pass she continues triumphantly to greet James with: "Mr. Herriot, haven't I made a difference to this dog!" (*ATBB,* 79).

Farmer Biggins is continually torn between his Yorkshire closeness with money and his concern for the health of his animals. He informs James that he has a "cow gruntin' a bit," and James wants to make a professional call. But because that would bring a charge, Mr. Biggins vacillates—"Well ah don't know. She's maybe not as bad as all that" (*ATBB,* 224)—and the conversation continues for three pages with Biggins still undecided about whether to employ the veterinary's services.

The ever patient James finally puts the indecisive farmer out of his misery (or perhaps fully into it) by firmly announcing that he will call at three o'clock. Biggins is stunned, crestfallen, but resigned to his fate: a vet's bill (*ATBB,* 227).

Mrs. Tompkin is frail, poorly sighted, and over eighty. Her sole company is a silent budgie named Peter, whose beak needs clipping because the "poor little fellar can hardly eat with 'is long beak and I'm worried about him" (*ATBB,* 26). When Herriot slowly reaches into the cage, the terrified bird dies in his hand. Stricken with guilt and dismay, the compassionate Herriot, under the pretext of needing to take Peter to the surgery to do the clipping properly, scurries off with the tiny corpse to find a similar-looking live bird. He does so and brings off the kind deception, although the widow later comments: "You know, you woullldn't believe it. . . . He's like a different bird. . . . chattering to me all day long. It's wonderful wat cuttin' the beak can do" (*ATBB,* 264).

Compassion is Herriot's strong suit as both healer and human, particularly because the veterinary medicine he practiced as a young man was relatively primitive: "there was one thing which we vets of those days used to do which is sometimes neglected since the arrival of modern drugs; we attended to the comfort and nursing of the animals" (*ATBB,* 352). Herriot and the farmers would wrap new-born calves in sacks to keep them warm. Then the veterinary would inspect the sheds, plugging up holes, and piling bales of hay between the animals and the door.

Herriot is very proud of his discovery of a simple but effective aid to a sick animal's recovery. It is a procedure that derived from his palpable compassion for his charges. Farmer Kitson badly mauls a ewe when trying to perform a difficult delivery himself and then leaves the suffering animal in a corner to die. Herriot sees the beast and wants to treat her, but the parsimonious farmer says: "Nay, Nay, I don't want none o' that. It's ower with her—there's nowt you can do" (*ATBB,* 245). James asks that the ewe be put out of her

misery, and the farmer says he will, but James is sure the
animal will be left to "take her chance." When Kitson is not
looking, James surrepititiously injects the ewe with a massive
sedative dose that should quickly and painlessly kill the animal. On a subsequent visit Herriot sees the ewe alive and
well. Kitson says that the sheep slept for two days, and then
perplexedly remarks: "Ah'll tell tha, young man, you'd just
think she'd been drugged!" (*ATBB*, 250). Herriot realizes
that the ewe survived not because of therapy but because he
stopped her pain and gave her stressless time to heal naturally.
Although he cannot explain it rationally, James realizes that
preventing the shock of great pain can help save an animal
from death. Herriot has a bad time with the suffering of the
living, and his compassion is not limited to animals.

The hard-working Frank Metcalf was not born a Yorkshire
farmer. He had been "a steelworker from Middlesbrough"
(*ATBB*, 301), and it seems that despite his back-breaking
labor, love for the land, and exquisite care of his small dairy
herd, fate rejects him, and the spirit of the region casts him
out. The accidental purchase of a diseased cow fatally infects
his herd with brucellosis. Neither Herriot's professional ministrations nor a quack's nostrum are able to stem the tide of
animal death in the days before antibiotics. Frank must pack
up, sell out, and return to the steelworks. It is like an unjust
penal sentence. Herriot never hears from Frank again, but he
also never forgets him, for every time he sees the "little new
byre" Frank had lovingly built for his milk cows, he feels "a
tug at my heart. . . . It was all that was left of a man's dream"
(*ATBB*, 310).

Herriot's attitudes toward the various classes in the pre–
World War II society he is describing in *All Things Bright and
Beautiful* do not differ from those of *All Creatures Great and
Small* except that he does not disparage the nouveau riche who
have brought their fortunes to rural Yorkshire in order to live
a gentrified life. The old, accepted gentry are treated with the
usual deference and courtesy so that Colonel Bosworth

D.S.O., M.C., for example, whose cat has been run over, is described in heroic terms:

> Most people had to look up at Colonel Bosworth with his lean six feet three inches and his tough soldier's face. . . . I saw quite a lot of him, not only when he came to the surgery but out in the country where he spent most of his time hacking along the quiet roads around Darrowby on a big hunter with Cairn terriers trotting behind. I liked him. He was a formidable man but he was unfailingly courteous and there was a gentleness in him which showed in his attitude to his animals (*ATBB,* 198).

This description of the good old soldier—officer class, built and born to lead, is stereotypical of course, derived from an ancient English literary convention going back to Chaucer's "parfit, gentil knight." Bosworth has a minor part in the text, but Herriot seems to feel that the landscape is incomplete without the presence of someone like a country squire right out of the nineteenth-century novels of Robert Smith Surtees: a well-born, well-bred, true English gentleman, the paragon so beloved and emulated by ex-colonials.

Closer to the common experience and to reality are the Flaxtons, middle class, the wife's "little round face with its shining tight cap of blue-black hair seemed to illumine the place like a beacon" (*ATBB,* 251). She smiles all the time; her baby is beautiful; the lapdog poodle, Penny, is ill but well behaved; and the husband, undescribed, is in the background. Herriot's baldly asserts: "They were the kind of people I liked to see" (*ATBB,* 253). The Flaxtons are a small genteel, Anglo-Saxon family, ostensibly local, but certainly "acceptable" people, unthreatening neighbors, and the "right sort."

The narrator, like all of us, is a prisoner of received values and acquired biases but, although sometimes condescending to those permanently residing on the lower rungs of British society's well-built ladder, he is never cruel or disrespectful.

The Dimmocks (Wight picks the name; are we to hear dim
and ox in it?) live in one of a "row of decaying cottages"
(*ATBB*, 287). Unlike the Flaxtons they speak with a heavy
Yorkshire dialect. "Mum" and "Dad, a diminutive figure,"
have eleven children, from a boy in his early teens to an infant,
and one more is on the way. Dad "had never done any work
within living memory" (*ATBB*, 288), and as hardworking,
middle-class Herriot recounts jealously, he spends his time
"roaming interestedly around the town by day and enjoying a
quiet beer and a game of dominoes in a corner of the Four
Horse Shoes by night" (*ATBB*, 288). Dad, something of a
Mr. Micawber, carries a walking stick "which gave him an air
of dignity and he always walked briskly and purposefully as
though he were going somewhere important" (*ATBB*, 289).
Mr. Dimmock is as much a stereotype as Colonel Bosworth.
He represents the "undeserving poor" on the dole, living off
the taxes paid by the middle class, irresponsible in reproductive sex, and so on. Even their injured dog Bonzo fits into the
representation: he is large, shaggy, of "indeterminate breed,"
and sits on a "ragged" blanket.

Yet Herriot is genuinely fond of the Dimmocks, despite the
implied disapproval of their lifestyle and the fact that they
never actually pay for his services. We are amused by them
too but perhaps only because we assume the heightened perspective that the narrator leads us to. We do not see the
children hungry for food as they must often be while their
father spends or mooches in the pub, and we do not see how
beset Mum must be, pregnant, and eleven other children to
care for in a tiny row cottage, probably a three- or four-room
accommodation. But a Herriot text is an exercise in nostalgic
memory, and therefore, true to the genre, the focus must be
fuzzy about the edges.

Like all five of Herriot's memoirs, *All Things Bright and
Beautiful* is a very funny book. The humor primarily comes

from situation, character, or a combination of both, not from epigrammatic language. In other words there are funny people and amusing situations, and sometimes funny people in amusing situations, and sometimes, as with Mr. Dimock or Mr. Pickersgill, they are just funny to see or listen to. The humor is enhanced through the age-old, sturdy technique of interstratifying comic moments and passages of sentiment or pathos; for humor, though created in a literary text by words of course, is ultimately a matter of emotion. Herriot's skill as a humorist is not as a wit kindling intellectual satisfaction but as a storyteller using character and situation to create surprising moments of pleasurable tension that are slowly or violently released, as air may be from a balloon, and then concluded by punch-line endings.

Two major themes structure the text: the ambivalence of progress, and, carried over from *All Creatures Great and Small,* the notion that humans serve God and nature best when they exercise wise, compassionate dominion and stewardship over other living things. Science and technology bring material increase to many (though not to all), decrease body-breaking labor, promote egalitarianism, defeat ignorance through access to information, and make possible longer and healthier lives for humans and animals. But progress also leaves much that is worthwhile behind: comity between the sexes, respect for life in general, the comfort of knowing one's place in the old feudal order, the sense of being a part of an old culture and community whose fellow members are ready and willing to stand by us in times of stress and to share with us, resignedly and stoically, a common destiny. Herriot appreciates modernity, but nevertheless he longs for the old ways, not only in human relations but within the archetypal partnership of humans and domesticated beasts. We are to give them food and care and often love in exchange for their services, their products, and, at an appropriate time, their lives for our food. Mechanization in such forms as tractors, factory farms, or corporate agribusiness are outside of that ancient compact.

Herriot lovingly allegorizes the best in the relationship of people to their working animals in the poignant story of Cliff Tyreman the "old horseman" (*ATBB,* 160–70). It is really the story of the disappearance of the animal that, in the long history of Western civilization, has worked the hardest for humans: the draft horse. That beast was also the mainstay of the veterinary profession for centuries. The tractor replaced the draft horse, and though a person can appreciate, value, and respect the internal combustion engine, one cannot love it, for it does not share with us a heart, breath, food, and affection. Cliff has the obsolete skill of masterly handling of the huge, potentially lethal workhorses. When James must humanely destroy Badger, Cliff's last old charge, the scene is heartwrenching (*ATBB,* 169–70). For Herriot has also had to end "the sweet core of Cliff Tyreman's life" (*ATBB,* 170). But the human spirit in those who live close to the land is nothing if not resilient. The seventy-year-old Cliff is last seen mounting the iron seat of a roaring tractor, shouting that he is not afraid of learning "summat new. I'm nobbut a lad yet!" (*ATBB,* 170).

The farmer, the pet owner, the veterinarian, together must exercise humane stewardship. In the suffering that Herriot sees and spends his life attempting to assuage, is the great, perennial challenge to all our humanity. Our response to suffering is ultimately how, as societies and individuals, we are to be judged.

All things bright and beautiful are left behind in the sad end of the memoir, the departure from the Peaceable Kingdom to the World at War. Herriot the storyteller is saying goodbye to the happy recollections of contented bachelorhood, pleasurable sexual anxiety, and the heady days of youthful love and success. War is a harsh, strict, and irresistible maturer of the young. He thought it was "the end of everything" (*ATBB,*

378). It was not. He would return to a changed but fortunately still recognizable way of life, and he; his family; his friends; and the people of the Pennines, dales, moors, and fells would strive to preserve that way and the physical world on which it thrived: "It was only the beginning."

5

All Things Wise and Wonderful

All Things Wise and Wonderful is the darkest in tone of the five Herriot memoirs, and for good reason: one of the frames of the text is the perspective of World War II. As Richard R. Lingeman points out: "niceness still triumphs, but this time around it's a near thing."[1] Of course the war against fascism was itself a near thing. Herriot's war, as shall be seen, was a sorry fiasco, a fact that accounts for some degree of somberness in the total text.

Like the relative caliginousness of tone, the narrative framing of the text is also unique in the five memoirs. First, the narrator is speaking for the author from the position of middle age in the early 1970s. Second, Herriot is recalling his RAF service in World War II. Third, while in the miseries of wartime separation from Helen, his practice, and his beloved Yorkshire, he daydreams, recollects, and reminisces about events in his early Darrowby days, the late 1930s, and the beginning of the fearsome next decade. The technique is difficult. Wight will attempt it again piecemeal and halfheartedly in *The Lord God Made Them All* and then give up on it. The multiple framing of this time-traveling text reminds us that a memoir as autobiography has its own relevance as a prismatic distortion of experience filtered through cerebral cells. For example, we shall see how the attitudes toward World War II in *All Things Wise and Wonderful* are those of the 1970s, not of the early 1940s.

In *All Things Wise and Wonderful* the reader as narratee is required to work harder, imaginatively, and to have a considerable degree of perspicacity as he or she is expected to internalize facilely the triple narration. The plan strains, the Herriot formula-plots with their carefully built suspense and quick surprise endings roll on, and the structure groans, but it all works.

Although the meat of the text is, as expected, the smorgasbord spread of events in Herriot's pre—world War II days in Yorkshire and the honest description of veterinary life, the primary narrative is that of Herriot's wartime service, which is mostly depicted in the opening lines or paragraphs of the forty-eight chapters in the 432-page book. Sometimes, however, toward the end of the narrative, whole chapters are devoted to the wartime experience. The strain sometimes occurs when Herriot, ostensibly to ward off loneliness and military boredom, tries to tie in recollections of service events with earlier, prewar events in his professional or personal life.

For example, when reviewing his copy of *Black's Veterinary Dictionary* in his barracksroom in St. John's Wood, he reaches the letter *C* and the word *castration*. This immediately reminds him of an Irish agricultural worker named Rory who was apprehensive over Herriot's fast and free-swinging use of his castrating blade as it hovered near Rory's trouser crutch. From a nine-line introduction a four-page story ensues.[2] This awkward transaction eventually tires the reader, who sotto voce mutters: "Oh come on. Just tell the tale." Yet the idea that a serviceman involved in physically exhausting, seemingly meaningless effort, in a dehumanizing environment, might indulge in a long, serialized wartime dream of peace is quite plausible.

Herriot even returns to his Scottish boyhood when he recalls leaving behind the smoke, dirt, and grit of Glasgow, to camp with school chums at beautiful Rosneath: "When I closed my eyes I could see the little pine-wood behind the tent and the green hillside running down to the burn and, far below, the long blue mirror of the Gareloch glinting under the great mountains of Argyl. They have desecrated Rosneath and the Gareloch now, but to me as a boy, it was a fairyland which led me into the full wonder and beauty of the world" (*ATWW,* 215). Herriot's Wordsworthian love of, and aesthetic need for, experience in the natural world obviously developed early in his life.

All Things Wise and Wonderful seems either an ironic title for this collection of memoirs or a line of hope that there was some inscrutable intelligence behind, and some plausible meaning and utility in, his military service. Another gloss of the title is that it ignores the war frame and refers to the prewar Darrowby tales, which, after all, constitute the bulk of the text, the product the reader expects and is buying.

The main subject of *All Things Wise and Wonderful* is Herriot's attempt to serve his country in wartime by becoming a pilot, while he tries to maintain contact with pregnant Helen as she is about to give birth to their first child, and also while he strives to keep "The Peaceable Kingdom" and his work skills alive in heart and mind. James Herriot's military service is presented as a mistake and as a failure. A country veterinarian could have remained in reserve occupation helping hard-pressed British agriculture feed a population that suffered extreme food shortages caused by the effective German submarine blockade. Instead of this rational decision, Herriot enlists as an aircrewman in the RAF, ostensibly out of patriotism or need to prove "manhood," although he never directly states this.

Paradoxically, the less-serious Tristan would seem to be the one to do something romantically foolish, quixotic, and dangerous like enlisting as an aircrewman, which, after the severe air losses in the Battle of Britain, was the only military posting open to men in reserve occupations that the government saw as equally important to the war effort as general military service. But Tristan, unlike James and Siegfried, waits out the call to arms, continues the vital practice as long as he can, and then winds up serving usefully as a veterinary in the British Army Veterinary Corps in the Middle East. We never learn what Siegfried or Donald V. Sinclair, presumably his real-life counterpart, actually did during his years in the RAF.

All Things Wise and Wonderful begins three days after *All Things Bright and Beautiful* leaves off. Herriot is in London being bawled at by a drill corporal. He is a part of a "gasping, panting column of men" who have reeled through the streets of the city "with never a sign of a park anywhere" (*ATWW*, 1). Already, Herriot feels dehumanized and part of a herd. A most remarkable aspect of the military service frame of the narrative is that Herriot becomes a herd animal, one of a great mass of young men, all looking alike in their identical uniforms, as if bred to uniformity, and all subject to the control and ministrations of more powerful beings. Even their lives are held at the whim of their masters, by whom they may be led to slaughter. Thus, a major theme of this darker tome is: military life, although it may sometimes be necessary, is patently absurd, dehumanizing, and an insult to humanity.

Grotesquely, the new recruit Herriot and his mates eat in the London Zoo, their meals "made interesting by the chatter of monkey and the roar of lions" (*ATWW*, 3). They march and march and run and run, with drill instructors as "herders." The London fog Herriot encounters is a metaphor for the fog of wartime military life that engulfs enlisted personnel, who seldom know where they are going and what will happen to them: "The fog swirled over the heads of the marching men; a London fog, thick, yellow, metallic on the tongue. I couldn't see the head of the column, only the swinging lantern carried by the leader" (*ATWW*, 10).

An inept RAF dentist, whom Herriot ironically calls the "Butcher," savages James's mouth; he chisels a perfectly useful

tooth out by banging on the tool with a mallet, and leaves a
needless gap. The suffering veterinarian thinks: "I had always
wondered how young horses felt when I knocked wolf teeth
out of them. Now I knew" (*ATWW, 28*). So quickly does
military life cause one to empathize with other animal life.
Later on Herriot describes a typical military sick call after
mindless regulations order all windows nailed open in winter
to toughen the men, which causes almost all of Herriot's unit
to come down with bronchitis. The ill men shuffle into a
corridor, bullied and driven by a bawling sergeant. "I looked
at the young men huddled there, white-faced and trembling.
Most of them were coughing and spluttering and one of them
clutched his abdomen as though he had a ruptured appendix"
(*ATWW, 130*). The ill men are marched off "nearly a mile
through the rain to the sick quarters in another hotel"
(*ATWW, 130*). The unstated but palpable fact is that Herriot
the veterinarian and most of the farmers he served treated sick
beasts with more consideration, skill, and compassion than he
and his comrades receive from military medicine.

Herriot learns what many a young man experiences on
almost a daily basis in any large city in the world: being
bullied and pushed around by police. When a military policemen treats him as if he were less than human, he thinks: "It
brought home to me something which had been slowly dawning on me ever since I joined the Air Force; that I had been
spoiled for quite a long time now. Spoiled by the fact that I
had always been treated with respect because I was a veterinary
surgeon, a member of an honourable profession. And I had
taken it entirely for granted" (*ATWW, 9*).

Herriot was only married a few months before his call up,
but clearly he very much enjoyed and appreciated married life.
One of the fine, nonpatriarchal, iterative values in the Herriot
canon is that the author never denigrates family or proffers
pejorative wisecracks or jokes at the expense of his marriage or
any other in which he observes mutual respect between partners. In the first few days of service Herriot realizes: "I like

women better than men" (*ATWW,* 31). Naïvely perhaps, and
with that touch of Victorianism that is part of his charm,
Herriot proclaims: "Women are gentler, softer, cleaner, alto-
gether nicer things and I, who always considered myself one
of the boys, had come to the surprising conclusion that the
companion I wanted most was a woman" (*ATWW,* 31). The
perspective is perhaps partly that of a boy-child recalling sense
memory of maternal care, and of course there is the element of
sexual longing by a young man suddenly deprived of regular
sex with his wife. He neglects the possibility that women
herded like wartime recruits, or in concentration camps, or in
prisons might not be any "gentler, softer, or cleaner" than
men in those situations. It should also be noted that Herriot
is quick to say that he always considered himself "one of the
boys" to forestall any possible assumption on the part of the
reader that he was in the least effeminate or effete.

Although genuinely adoring women, Herriot, a narrator
constructed out of midcentury male values and attitudes, refers to his wife and Mrs. Zoe Bennett as "girls" (*ATWW,*
199). In describing his own sentimentality toward pets he
states: "I have always been as soppy as any old lady over my
pets" (*ATWW,* 195). In the hospital he wonders "what it was
in a girl's character that made her go in for the arduous life
of nursing?" (*ATWW,* 355), not considering that many of
the "girls" would have liked opportunities to be physicians
instead.

When AC2 Herriot has the duty to awaken the barracks
by means of "the sadistic pleasure of rattling the dustbin lids
and shouting 'Wakey-wakey!' along the corridors," he does
not object so much to the cursing and obscenities he hears but
to "the extraordinary abdominal noises issuing from the dark
rooms" (*ATWW,* 31). The farting, much of it purposely done,
reminds Herriot that the human is an animal too, unsanitary,
primitive, smelly, stupid seeming, and unpleasant when
closely confined and manifestly micro-managed. There is little
doubt that military service brings out a touch of the misan-

thrope in this otherwise most understanding and forgiving of
men. Perhaps that is the reason why *All Things Wise and
Wonderful* is dedicated "To my dogs, Hector and Dan."

With indoctrination and basic training ending in London,
Herriot, worried about the confinement of Helen and the birth
of their first child, awaits assignment to an Initial Training
Wing somewhere in Britain. There he will spend months
learning principles of flight, transmission codes, and navigation, before being taught to fly and, with luck, becoming an
RAF pilot, apparently a dream he feels a little foolish to
mention thirty years after the fact.

Posted to the Yorkshire resort of Scarborough, Herriot is
much nearer to Helen than he expected to be. Untold hours of
drilling and physical training ensue along with navigation
classes. Herriot finds, like so many recruits who are not broken
or injured by the running in winter and the calisthenics, that
he has been honed into the best physical shape of his life. At
the same time, Helen is continually on his mind. He even
experiences a sympathetic pregnancy, convinced to this day
that he "carried" their son (*ATWW,* 87). Finally he risks
serious trouble by going absent without leave to see Helen,
and he gets away with it. A second "French leave" brings
him to Darrowby serendipitously just minutes after Helen is
delivered by a midwife of a son, the Jimmy of later tales
(*ATWW,* 112). The veterinarian who has assisted the birth of
hundreds of animals is astonished by the sight of his newborn
child and insists on being shown other newborns to make sure
that the "brick red . . . bloated, dissipated" looking creature
with his tongue hanging out of the corner of his mouth is "all
right" (*ATWW,* 113–14).

Some six months after induction, Herriot is promoted to
leading aircraftsman, and with his *Black's Veterinary Dictionary*
in his pack, he is shipped to Shropshire not yet to undergo
flight training but, physically fit as he is, to take a tough-

ening-up course. Hundreds of men are milling around. It appears that the RAF has far more men than, at this relatively late stage of the war, it can process into air crews. Then in the strangest of anomalies Herriot makes his sole contribution to the British war effort in his two years of military service, and he does it on a farm!

The airmen have been kept busy digging an alleged reservoir out of a hill. Local farmers need labor, and airmen are asked to volunteer to help bring in the harvest. James volunteers and is assigned to a Farmer Edwards, under whose tutelage he learns empirically what he had previously observed: "farming was the hardest way of all of making a living" (*ATWW*, 216). Herriot and some mates do the backbreaking work of "stooking" (collecting and standing sheaves of wheat).

James does not mention to Mr. Edwards that he is a veterinarian, and the farmer is too polite to ask his temporary help what their civilian occupations were. One afternoon the farmer is struggling vainly with a cow's breech birth, and to his amazement Herriot easily delivers the calf alive and well, simultaneously teaching Edwards how to deal with such a problem. Finally, James tells the bewildered farmer that he is a qualified veterinarian. Mr. Edwards is delighted: "You young bugger! You kept that dark, didn't you?" (*ATWW*, 222).

That is the contribution. Although Herriot does not realize it at the time, the sum total of his war work is one live calf, for fate has a cruel trick in store for the patriot apparently so anxious to prove his manhood and fly in combat.

From Shropshire's plains Herriot is dispatched at last to flying school at Windsor. His spirits rise as he is issued a very different uniform, the garb of the new trade he is apprenticing: "the baggy flying suit . . . the sheepskin boots and the gloves," then the "leather helmet and goggles." Finally, with understated pride and usual Herriot skill at observing and describing procedures, he says: "I fastened on my parachute passing the straps over my shoulders and between my legs and buckling them against my chest before shuffling out of the flight hut on to the long stretch of sunlit grass" (*ATWW*, 226). He is learning to fly at last. Despite the difficulties of the course, his sadness at missing the babyhood of his then only child, his fear that his vertigo will affect his flying skills, and his own feelings of insecurity because he is seven or eight years older than almost all the other trainees, an old married man to the eighteen-year-olds, he solos his Tiger Moth trainer successfully.

The triumphant solo flight is, meaning no pun, the high point of the book and the climax of Herriot's military career. Herriot forgets the drill and gets lost on the flight but finally locates a landmark, makes it back to the field, and executes a perfect landing (*ATWW*, 308–11). He is the third in his flight of fifty to successfully solo.

The aviator's fall comes fast, and all the rest is anticlimax. Graded pilot and posted to Manchester after flying school, he is told that he must have an operation. Apparently, Herriot has had surgery before, and for some reason "the thing is opening up again and needs attention" says the medical officer (*ATWW*, 350). His comrades leave for overseas and the war, while he must immediately report to a hospital near Hereford where he is operated on for a condition never revealed in the text. Coincidentally, the anesthesiologist turns out to be an old high school friend who asks the key question of the book: "what the devil is a vet doing in the RAF?" (*ATWW*, 354). The answer is left for the reader to fill in.

Recuperating and in hospital garb, Herriot is embarrassed because people think he has been wounded in action. After a stay in a convalescent home near Leominster, he is sent back to Manchester where he learns that he "can no longer be classed as 100% physically fit" (*ATWW*, 372). It is another World War II catch-22. He has had to have an operation to make him fit, but because he has had the operation, he is classified unfit to do the work the military has so expensively trained him for. Implicit in *All Things Wise and Wonderful* is a distinct distrust for the diagnoses and treatments of medical and dental practitioners, at least in a military context. Herriot seems to imply that veterinarians, all in all, do a better job with animals than MDs and dentists do with human patients.

So, after all his struggle and hard work, after all he gave up to answer the call, Herriot has been officially downgraded physically and is ineligible to fly. To add insult to injury, the RAF does not know what to do with him. Poor James feels "intensely lonely and cut off" (*ATWW,* 373). The sounds and sights around him all conspire to remind him of his comrades and the experiences they shared. Herriot sums up his failure: "I hadn't fired a shot in anger. I had peeled mountains of potatoes, washed countless dishes, shovelled coke, mucked out pigs, marched for miles, drilled interminably, finally and magically learned to fly and now it was all for nothing (*ATWW,* 373).

Instead of doing a logical thing with Herriot for once and sending him back to his veterinary practice, the RAF assigns him to a warehouse where he watches over mounds of shirts. Previously, psychologists have given him a series of aptitude tests "discovering" that this individual, who can't do a thing to fix his car, has an outstanding "mechanical aptitude" (*ATWW,* 379). Nonplussed at his revelation that he has minus mechanical ability, the psychologists ask him if he would like to be a meteorologist, and the ever agreeable James says yes. But of course there is no chance of his becoming a meteorologist. Instead he is "warehoused" in stores.

Finally, in one of two requisite scenes, Herriot is demobilized. "They had taken away my blue uniform and fitted me with a 'demob suit', a ghastly garment of stiff brown serge with purple stripes which made me look like an old-time gangster" (*ATWW,* 431). In the second requisite scene, James Herriot, now older, wiser, and sadder, has a second coming to Darrowby. The last leg of the long journey home is in "the same rattling little vehicle that had carried me to my first job those years ago. The driver was the same too, and the time between seemed to melt away as the fells began to rise again

from the blue distance in the early light and I saw the familiar
farmhouses, the walls creeping up the grassy slopes, the fringe
of trees by the river's edge" (*ATWW,* 431). Let out of the bus
at the square, he grips his cardboard case, and as many a
veteran if not a veterinarian has done, he sets off like an old
soldier—"left-right, left-right"—for Helen, for Jimmy, and
for home.

In *All Things Wise and Wonderful,* more clearly than elsewhere in the Herriot canon of memoirs, the reader can identify
an essential construct of persona that subjoins and mitigates
the image of benign healer and provides the base on which
much of the Herriot humor rests. Herriot is a perennial outsider, frequent loser, sometimes victim, butt of jokes (especially his own), a Good Soldier (Airman) Schweik driven by
his misery to howling "woof! woof!" at night at the window
of his commanding officer (*ATWW,* 111). He plays the dis-
arming shlemiel who seems to say: "laugh at ineffectual, in-
nocuous, unprepossessing, vulnerable, unthreatening me,
although I may really not worth the effort. I am a spectator
not a player. I am only a lucky fool with a good wife." However, all of this complexity, double-helix-like, is superimposed on, and entwined with, a core belief in his self-worth,
compassion, professional competence, and capacity to love in
the best personal but nonlibidinal sense of the word: to take
responsibility for others, to risk for those loved ones, to care
for them above self.

Almost from birth Wight himself was an "other," an outsider. Born in England, he and his English parents were outsiders in Glasgow, as Wight's early school chums would have
made clear to him. Likewise, the Herriot recollections of
childhood contain both comic and pathetic humiliations: the
tram conductor in Glasgow who humiliated him on his first
date by giving him his change all in halfpennies, forcing him
to pay for cinema tickets by counting out a pile of coppers
while the queue waited (*AC,* 402); the Scottish horse that
demolishes his adolescent hubris by grabbing and hoisting

him aloft by his shoulder in front of a crowd of people (*AC*, 107). No wonder Herriot likes to leave horse work to Siegfried.

Coming to Yorkshire from Glasgow, he is a young Scot in one of England's most remote and conservative areas. There he must prove himself professionally and as an ethical person and as a man. He is neither confident nor prepossessing. As stated earlier, winning the hand of Helen signifies his acceptance among the dalespeople and perhaps even acceptance by the very land itself, for Helen is both of the land and symbolically the fertile locus itself. His quixotic enlistment in the RAF, unnecessary as he is in a reserve occupation, is a gesture to ensure acceptance as a young man working among men who served king and country in the 1914–1918 war.

Alas, in the air force he is an outsider again, older than the eighteen-year-olds with whom he serves, and with the responsibilities of husband and father-to-be. Accepted finally and successful as a pilot-trainee, his medical problem isolates him once more, and he becomes a square peg in a service of round holes. Then he joyously returns to Yorkshire, but he is starting all over again, and the reader will see in the next volume, *The Lord God Made Them All*, if Herriot's sacrifice of two years or so of his life to the idea of patriotism finally brings him the acceptance he seeks.

Returning to the Darrowby stories, we find some of Herriot's best animal tales in *All Things Wise and Wonderful*. Wight has certainly not exhausted his material at this point. Wisely, he opens with the poignant story of Blossom the cow, a good, old beast whose hanging teats are continually trampled and cut by other cows and her own hooves. She has served Farmer Dakin long and well, and he loves her, but he feels it is time to send her to the knackers. The farmer won't let her be struck or driven, and she follows the herdsman by voice commands, but, unseen, she turns back to her byre, and the farmer does not have the heart to have her butchered. He comes up with a solution that brings tears to the reader's eyes.

He will put her in an empty old stable, where, alone, she will be safe. He rationalizes his emotional response: "she can live in there where there's nobody to stand on 'er awd tits. . . . After all them years she doesn't owe me a thing. . . . Main thing is she'ss come 'ome"(*ATWW*, 8).

As the lead-off reminiscence the tale of Blossom is the objective correlative for the emotion of compassion that is so central to the Herriot canon. Humans must care about their animal charges if we ever can expect them to care about their fellow humans. Aficionados of Herriot stories understand this implicitly. Wight knows what he is doing to bind his audience to him in commonality of purpose: he illustrates how to extend human caring, kindness, and concern to animals, for they are all ours—to love or destroy. In a *Life Magazine* interview the author said: "There is a big bond between animal lovers. They all seem to speak the same language."[3] It is not unrelated to the Herriot appeal that most Western men and women have chosen to open their homes to animals and live their lives in their animals' company as their ancestors have done for fifteen millennia.

Another example of compassion in the text, this time exercised by James and Tristan, is their operation on a poor old shepherd's suffering dog, stricken with painfully turned-in eyelids causing the eyelashes to rub continually against the beast's eyeballs. The community of pub men contribute money, and the difficult operation is a success. The dog cannot say thanks, and Mick's old master never fully realizes what has been done, but significant male bonding between men of different life stations has taken place in a pub, and more important, an animal is saved from continual suffering (*ATWW*, 121–28).

Later, when some monstrous person is poisoning dogs, and Herriot is reminding us through the World War II frame of how much evil their is in the world, he struggles successfully to save the life of guide dog so vital to the existence of Fergus's blind master (*ATWW*, 142–44). Then Herriot, in his reverence for life, talks a farmer into allowing him to partially amputate Nellie the cow's foot to save her life (*ATWW*, 278–82).

When Herriot particularizes a farm animal with a name, the compassion flows in him, in most of the farmers involved, and in the reader. As a conservator Herriot is unhappy when dairy farmers begin to run milk-producing factories, where the cows are no longer thought of as individuals with names and concomitant personalities, but as mere numbers on ear tags. When an old man dies and the widow is not well enough to walk their dog, Herriot goes out of the way when walking his dog Sam to give old Nip a regular run (*ATWW*, 377). And when James must put down a dog, he speaks to him: " 'Good lad, good old Theo' I muttered, and stroked the face and ears again and again as the little creature slipped peacefully away. Like all vets I hated doing this, painless though it was, but to me there has always been a comfort in the knowledge that the last thing these helpless animals knew was the sound of a friendly voice and the touch of a gentle hand" (*ATWW*, 325). Do you and I dare hope for such compassion from our final care giver?

Small animals are also individualized and given special anthropomorphic characteristics. Judy is a "nurse dog" who watches over and comforts sick farm animals (*ATWW*, 355–59). Oscar is "a cat-about-town" who likes to attend public meetings, which may indicate that he is not so anthropomorphic (*ATWW*, 423–25). The stray cat Debbie instinctively or intelligently carries her kitten in her mouth to a safe haven just before Debbie herself dies (*ATWW*, 79–85).

Herriot reflects once more on the rigid sexual mores of rural Yorkshire as he contrasts them with what he sees and hears in the military. His bald conclusion: "one of the least permissive societies in the history of mankind was the agricultural community of rural Yorkshire in the thirties. Among the farmers anything to do with sex or the natural functions was unmentionable" (*ATWW,* 157), and he illustrates with the tale of a farmer totally unable to mention "unmentionables" (*ATWW,* 156–70).

Major characters continue their stories in *All Things Wise and Wonderful:* Siegfried, Tristan, and Helen of course. The affluent colleague Gordon Bennett and his beautiful wife Zoe appear again, and once more Gordon gets James sick drunk. Helen must drive her inebriate husband home. Although the episode is amusing, and at the expense of the weakness in James's character when he is urged to drink too much and overeat, it is less funny this time. (*ATWW,* 193–204).

Minor characters return. Lord Hulton, referred to in *All Creatures Great and Small* (35), is now fleshed out into a loveable, aristocratic eccentric who dresses like his farm laborers and works as hard as they do in the most menial of jobs like "plugging muck." (*ATWW,* 12). His democratic instincts and actions extend even to serving Herriot breakfast with his own hands after the veterinarian saves his "fine pedigree pig" (*ATWW,* 21). Lord Hulton is delightfully amusing and one of the least probable of Herriot's characters, but the author is partial to the titled holders of familial land and anxious to show that at least one of them is one of us.

Stewie Brannan, Siegfried's college friend and drinking buddy from *All Creatures Great and Small* (414–21), is brought back to the saga, permitting three episodes like those two with Angus Grier in *All Creatures Great and Small* (127–31; 210–14) that take Herriot away from Darrowby and briefly into an other practice. Stewie's practice is in a dingy West Riding of Yorkshire industrial town. He is married with six children, and Siegfried asks James to take over Stewie's shoestring practice for two weeks so the impoverished, struggling veterinarian can take his family on a seaside vacation in Blackpool. The practice consists of the treating of pets of impecunious working class people in an underequipped surgery, where the examination table keeps collapsing (*ATWW,* 166).

Herriot has a most satisfying opportunity to save a badly injured dog, struck by an auto, despite the lack of sulfanilamide and other appropriate medicines and instruments in Stewie's supplies. He uses a crude technique discovered in the Spanish Civil War (1936–1939) and about which he has read. Despite the professional triumph Herriot is most happy to return to the idyllic Darrowby practice. Herriot has used the Stewie Brannan episodes to contrast, unfavorably, a poor city practice, which specializes in small animals, with a successful country practice, like Siegfried Farnon's, which primarily cares for large animals. Herriot is pleased with the hand fate dealt him.

The veterinary discourse continues to serve the text as an architectonic in the function of iterative imagery. Herriot's treatments and apparatus include silver nitrate, oxide of mercury, Ichthyol (for skin diseases), an ophthalmoscope, zinc oxide plaster, antileptospiral serum (for spirochets), prolan (hormone), apomorphine (emetic), arsenical tablets, and mixed macterin (antidistemper).

Diseases and ailments include clostridium septique, actinobacillosis (bacilli infection), varicocele (spermatic cord veins enlargement), keratitis sicca (inflamed, dry cornea), pigmentary keratitis, entropion (inversion of eyelids), distichiasis (extra row of eyelashes rubbing eyeball), suppurative arthritis, leptospirosis, phosphorous poisoning, rumenotomy (opening first stomach), liver fluke (worms), peritonitis (inflammation of abdominal membrane), swine erysipelas (infectious skin disease), asphyxia (deprivation of oxygen or excess of oxygen, which can lead to unconsciousness), displacement of the abomasum (fourth stomach), St. Vitus' dance (chorea: nervous disease), photophobia, rumenal atony (lack of tone), and mucopurulent discharge.

The new animal anatomy lesson cites the orbital cavity (eye socket), interphalangeal joints, pedal (foot) bones, coronet (upper margin of horse's hoof), patella (kneecap), corpus luteum (hormone-secreting body), omentum (peritoneum fold), flexors (muscles for bending), extensors (muscles for extending), sternohyoid and omohyoid muscles, cotyledons (villi on placenta), optic papilla (where optic nerve fibers leave eyeball), and thoracic (chest) glands.

Although *All Things Wise and Wonderful* is the least upbeat of the five memoirs because Herriot's narration of his ineffective and wasteful wartime service is the text's subject-frame, and although Herriot's technique of self-portrayal as passive outsider and comic butt is more marked is the context of a generation of young people who have lost control of their lives, the book is not intended to, nor does it, leave the reader with a sense of defeat. First of all, Herriot survives the war unharmed. Then his Helen safely gives birth to their first child, and James is with her from the moments immediately after the delivery. Their love and commitment grows stronger despite the long separations. Herriot achieves a personal triumph in being designated a pilot. And his old life and the countryside he has grown to cherish await him at book's end.

Herriot's defeats in the service conflate with the victories in his practice, although the overriding triumph is, naturally, his solo flight (*ATWW,* 310). As always, Herriot modestly understates his veterinary successes, often giving nature or the good care of lay people top billing. Still, the cures corrrelate with Herriot's philosophical thesis that the life worth living is the useful one. Sometimes human beings are the recipients of these cures. Andrew Vine is a depressed bachelor with a dog going blind. He reminds Herriot of his deceased friend Paul Cotterell, a man so silently depressed that he committed suicide over the loss of his dog. Herriot's simple message of service is "Remember you've got a job to do with that dog" (*ATWW,* 336). Vine eventually realizes the foolishness of torturing oneself over what cannot be helped or changed. He no

longer will spend his days taking a mishap and beating himself
"over the head with it" (*ATWW*, 337).

Farmer Blackburn has turned his dairy into relatively big
business agriculture with "a seemingly endless succession of
bovine backsides protruding from tubular metal standings"
(*ATWW*, 313). He has called Herriot because a cow calving
has "summat amiss," but he is too busy meeting his productions schedule to help James as the young veterinarian treats
"Number Eighty-Seven." Despite the fact that workers are
bustling about everywhere, James is lonely, and he must talk
to the anonymous cow as she undergoes her difficult but successful delivery. No person sees or commends James's skillful
and caring effort. But James can smile to himself. He knows
what he has done. And in the end the busy, taciturn farmer
who, like so many men, cannot bring himself to praise, gives
James a breakfast egg and says: "Tell your missus to put this
in the frying pan" (*ATWW*, 318). The egg may be an unusual
signifier, but the sign is clear: well done! A grin and a
"friendly thump on the chest" accompany the act (*ATWW*,
318). Men will be men.

Dread of foot-and-mouth disease haunts the farmers and
veterinarians of Yorkshire. The first sign of an outbreak causes
an immediate slaughter and burning of infected carcasses with
a concomitant stopping of agricultural business in the affected
district. When one of Farmer Bailey's cows shows possible
symptoms of the disease, after an outbreak has seemingly been
controlled, Herriot is terrified that despite having taken thor-
ough preventative actions, he may have brought the infection
on a previous visit, and thus condemned the Bailey's valuable
herd. As he is about to call the Agricultural Ministry for
assistance, Mrs. Bailey mentions that she has had her one-
year-old infant vaccinated for smallpox (*ATWW*, 400) and
that she daily changes the dressing. Mrs. Bailey also milks the
cows. At the last minute James realizes that Mrs Bailey has
passed on cowpox, the source of smallpox vaccine, to the herd.
It is not serious. The herd will not have to be destroyed.

Herriot and the life force win another one, and the infant whose welfare depends on the health of the dairy herd will "never know how near his smallpox vaccination came to giving me heart failure" (*ATWW*, 402).

All Things Wise and Wonderful left the Herriot readership wondering about his life as adjusting veteran returned to routine days in the postwar world. The author obliged.

1. Sinclair's & Wight's (Farnon's & Herriot's) veterinary surgery in Thirsk. Courtesy Joan Eyeington.

2. Wight (Herriot) autographing books. Courtesy *Northern Echo*.

3. Herriot territory. Roulston Scar and Hood Hill
from the top of Sutton Bank. Courtesy Joan Eyeington.

4. Wight (Herriot) with fans. Courtesy *Northern Echo*.

5. Wight (Herriot) in front of the Parish Church
of St. Mary's, Thirsk. Courtesy British Tourist Authority.

6. Christopher Timothy as Herriot and friend.
Courtesy BBC Lionheart.

7. Yorkshire pig. Courtesy Joan Eyeington.

8. Sheep in Newtondale. Courtesy Joan Eyeington.

9. Christopher Timothy treating a bovine patient.
Courtesy BBC Lionheart.

6

The Lord God Made Them All

With the title *The Lord God Made Them All,* Wight completed the verse of Mrs. Cecil Frances Alexander's hymn and may have been signaling to his readers and himself that this fourth tome would conclude his Herriot memoirs. Of course, that would not prove to be the case; however, there is a certain feeling, in this text, of winding up, of potpourri, of gathering up odds and ends of experiences perhaps not previously remembered or thought worthy of inclusion in the earlier volumes, and there is the awkward, disjunctive, chronology of this fourth memoir. Simply put, the book fails in logical unity and jumps all over place and time more than in the other books. Herriot reminisces from about 1980. But at various times in the book he speaks of events in the late 1930s, the late 1940s, Lithuania and Poland in 1961, and Turkey in 1963. The result is occasional confusion. Is the veterinary tale interspersed with events in two journeys, taking place before the war, after the war, before marriage, after bachelorhood, in his apprenticeship, in his maturity, and so on?

In *All Things Wise and Wonderful,* the author successfully constructed a primary frame based on his World War II experiences in the RAF. *In The Lord God Made Them All,* he tries to emulate that procedure, but he does not have a single dramatic story powerful enough or long enough to sustain such a narrative structure, and so he chooses two brief incidents in his later life to form a successive double internal architectonic for the thirty-eight chapter, 373-page text. Eight chapters are devoted to the Lithuania (Soviet Union) trip in 1961 and three chapters to the trip to Turkey in 1963. The extended story chapters, interspersed with veterinary tales and stories of his growing children, are longer than the average chapters in the text.

First, however, Herriot's surprising, provocative opening chapter must take precedence in discussion. Herriot seems determined to test the loyalty of his fans as well as the strength of their stomachs, and to challenge possible criticism of his writing as saccharine, Pollyannaish, and juvenile-targeted. Chapter 1, after a single continuity sentence that ties the text to *All Things Wise and Wonderful,* is a flashback to pre-RAF days, in which the veterinarian is called to "nip some calves"[1] for Farmer Ripley with his Burdizzo bloodless castrator. Herriot does not spare the details. As a veterinary surgeon he is, of course, not bothered by either performing or visualizing the procedures, and he may be informing young readership that a veterinarian's work is not always merely stroking and comforting pussycats. However, some readers find themselves skimming over the details of the operation.

Chapter 1 also reinforces Herriot's proud conservatism. Farmer Ripley's gate was a menace to James before his military service, and the farmer had "guaranteed" to repair it. Upon his first postwar visit to the Ripley farm to "nip" some more calves, Herriot is bruised and cut by the unrepaired, wild-swinging gate. When Ripley is confronted with his broken promise, he hollowly "guarantees" once more to repair the gate. James, however, is not irked by the prevarication. He muses on the reason for his equanimity: "Perhaps it was because I'd been away from Yorkshire so long, seeing a world changing faster than I sometimes liked, but this homely sign of immutability tickled me. I chuckled. And then I began to laugh" (*LGMTA,* 14).

Near the end of the book, another example of Herriot's inherent conservatism occurs in the chapter in which he de-

implication of this conservative text is that the traditional division of marital duties and responsibilities is at least in part responsible for the continued happiness of this once financially poor young couple. Herriot unreservedly states his conservatism: "I have always abhorred change of any kind" (*ATBB,* 113).

James will unabashedly enjoy all the male privileges of a traditional Victorian marriage. Helen studies his comforts: "The neat pile of clothing laid out for me each morning; the clean, folded shirt and handkerchief and socks so different from the jumble of my bachelor days. And when I was late for meals, which was often, she served me with my food but instead of going off and doing something else she would down tools and sit watching me while I ate. It made me feel like a sultan" (*ATBB,* 311). James realizes that Helen has learned to provide her man with this degree of devoted service from her father for whom "she had catered gladly to his every wish in the happy acceptance that the man of the house was number one" (*ATBB,* 311–12). Even though his work is quite physically demanding, Herriot grows stouter under Helen's cooking so that the occasional farmer remarks: "By gaw, you've been on a good pasture, young man!" (*ATBB,* 313).

Helen's gender role as a Victorian model "good woman" is one in which she appears to be satisfied, but the reader must consider that it is Herriot's view of the marriage that we have to work with. "Life with 'James Herriot' " as narrated by Helen Alderson Herriot, written by Joan Danbury Wight, might be a very different set of tales indeed. Regardless, Herriot's Helen, the strong, doting, domestic, devoted wife-mother of young James is not a viable role model for today's young women. Rather, she is prototypical of a woman that contemporary feminism considers an anachronism. Yet she is a nostalgic, grandmotherly construct inseminated in the reader's mind and given life there.

Gallantly, or perhaps because it is more humorous this

way, Herriot portrays Helen as rock-steady and more mature than he depicts himself. The young, presoldiering Herriot is painted as a humble, diffident, socially unsure man with an ego that only asserts itself when he is sure of his diagnoses and ethical positions. He is also a bumbler in his marriage. When delegated by Helen to attend house sales so they can obtain badly needed furniture, cutlery, and crockery, he squanders their limited resources on such items as "a pair of brass candlesticks and a stuffed owl" as well as on "an ornate inkwell with a carved metal figure of a dog on it" (*ATBB,* 116). The great white elephant purchase is an 1858 edition of *The Geography of the World in Twenty-Four Volumes* that turns out to be almost impossible to get home to Darrowby from Leeds and is so moldy that it must be banished to the cellar to keep the air on the third floor breathable (*ATBB,* 123).

Herriot is modest about his importance in the world of veterinary science. A brilliant young veterinary student, Richard Carmody, works under Herriot for six months when James is still only an assistant to Siegfried. Carmody impresses the impoverished Herriot not only with his intellectual brilliance and self-assurance but also with his posh outfit: a "fine check suit and tweedy hat . . . shining brogues and pigskin case" (*ATBB,* 231). Working in field and barn with James disturbs Carmody's wardrobe but not his aplomb. He becomes a famous research scholar with a Ph.D., and when, after twenty years, James meets him once more at a professional banquet where Carmody is a guest of honor, James humbly refers to himself as "a happily obscure practitioner" in deference to his former apprentice's esteem (*ATBB,* 243).

Herriot's main personal difficulty, presented humorously of course, is with alcohol. Granville Bennett is a successful small-animal surgeon in a nearby city, whose state-of-the-art operating room, affluence, Bentley, single malt Scotch, and general lifestyle with his beautifully groomed wife, Zoe, James envies. Bennett's personality completely dominates James', and on each of three visits to Bennett, the older,

cries the foolish indulgence of Mr. and Mrs. Whithorn toward their dogs, an indulgence that makes them into spoiled, misbehaving pets. Herriot agrees with the milkman, Doug Watson, that the owners, not the pets, are at fault when they "never correct them, and they slobber over them all the time" (*LGMTA,* 347). The milkman lectures for Herriot: "A dog likes to obey. It gives them security" (*LGMTA,* 347). Herriot is really instructing his reading public not to be indulgent with their pets or their children. He is firmly on the side of reasonable discipline's being in the best interest of human or beast.

Chapter 1 also has an especially significant descriptive passage. The narration refers to the narrator's perception of his adopted province as he comprehended it once more upon his return from wartime service. He is gazing at a farm he has not seen for several years: "I looked back at the house and . . . felt a sense of peace. Like many of the older farms, Anson Hall had once been a noble manor. Hundreds of years ago some person of title had built his dwelling in a beautiful place. The roof looked ready to fall in and one of the tall chimney stacks leaned drunkenly to one side, but the mullioned windows, the graceful arch doorway and stately proportions of the building were a delight, with the pastures beyond stretching towards the green fells" (*LGMTA,* 11). The garden of Anson Hall once in its former glory "would have enclosed a cropped lawn with bright flowers, but now there were only nettles. Those nettles fascinated me, a waist-high jungle filling every inch of space between wall and house. Farmers are notoriously bad gardeners but Mr. Ripley was in a class by himself" (*LGMTA,* 11). Herriot is using his reintroduction to the Yorkshire farm as a metaphor for his thoughts about post–World War II England or all of Britain. The war veteran sees his country as a reclaimed ruined, once far more glorious than it is now, but still naturally beautiful, productive, and viable. Yorkshire is the microcosm of what for him was and still is the best of Britain.

The very funny chapter 26 is one of the most risqué in all

of the Herriot annals. In order to facilitate artificial insemina-
tion, Siegfried and James purchase an artificial vagina, "a tube
of hard, vulcanized rubber about eighteen inches long with a
lining of latex. There was a tap on the tube, and warm water
was run into this to simulate the temperature of a genuine
bovine vagina. On one end of the A.V. was a latex cone
secured by rubber bands and this cone terminated in a glass
tube in which the semen was collected" (*LGMTA*, 235–36).
James kneels down by a randy bull as the animal throws his
forelegs on top of the waiting cow's rump. James moves
quickly, of course, "as the penis emerged from the sheath I
grabbed it and poised the A.V. for action" (*LGMTA*, 237).
But the bull backs off, his dignity outraged. Both animal and
man try again. This time the beast attacks the veterinarian,
and James attempts to beat him off with blows from the
"A.V." Herriot observes: "I have often wondered since that
day if I am the only veterinary surgeon to have used an artificial vagina as a defensive weapon" (*LGMTA*, 238).

The bull is stunned and uncomprehending: "His instinct
told him that right about now he should be having a good
time, and yet all he was getting were raps on the nose"
(*LGMTA*, 238). When the elastic holding the latex lining
comes off, causing warm water to splash in the bull's eye, the
animal gives up. "In his experience of humans I was something new to him. I had taken intimate liberties with him in
the pursuit of his lawful duty" (*LGMTA*, 239). Fortunately,
Tristan, the old lady-killer, appears on the scene and manages
to bring off the retrieval of the semen.

The bloodiest scene in *The Lord God Made Them All* is the
dehorning episode in chapter 33. Herriot begins by explaining
the menace that cows' and bulls' horns pose to veterinarians,
farmers, and to other animals. With only the faintly restrained
glee of a Grand Guignol director, he describes the guillotine
initially used in the practice (*LGMTA*, 311–12). Then the
imperious Siegfried gets the idea to use hedge clippers and
drags James off to Albert the ironmonger's to try a pair of

powerful clippers on bamboo canes, while the poor Albert, ordered to "look sharp," holds them and watches the exuberant veterinarian wield the curved, sharp blades to within an inch of his fingers (*LGMTA*, 312). Herriot describes a massive and terrifying hemorrhage as a horn is cut: "Red jets fountained several feet in the air, spraying everything and everybody for yards around" (*LGMTA*, 314).

Clearly the author is reminding his adult audience and advising his young impressionable readership that the life of a veterinarian is often extremely unpleasant, bloody, dirty, stomach turning, physically exhausting, and dangerous.

The first of the two long, James Herriot abroad stories begins in 1961 when a former assistant, John Crooks, tells him of his occasional work as a veterinary attendant in the animal export business. Herriot is intrigued and envious, and Crooks offers to arrange a trip assignment for his old boss. Herriot jumps at the chance to accompany livestock to "Russia": "Book me in, John, It's really kind of you. Country vetting is fine but sometimes I feel I'm sliding into a rut. A trip to Russia is just what I need" (*LGMTA*, 35). Interestingly, Herriot accepts the assignment apparently without discussing with Helen his plan to leave her and their children behind while he has his adventure, even though the trip will transpire over their wedding anniversary. (Wight, of course, may have discussed the journey with Joan Wight, but that possibility is not evident in the text.)

Herriot's voyage, recounted as journal entries, is not to Russia per se but to the then Soviet state of Lithuania, and the old port of Memel, renamed by Russians as Klaipeda. He sails on a small Danish coaster with a cargo of sheep. Baltic storms do not upset his equilibrium or deter his appetite, and he proves to be a good sailor while the three-hundred-ton, *Iris Clausen* proves to be a great feeder. Herriot is somewhat naïve about historical facts and political conditions in what was the

Soviet Union (a term he does not use) during the Cold War. He calls the people he meets in Klaipeda "Russians," when they probably are Lithuanians; he suspects that populations have been moved; and he seems surprised at the degree of port security he encounters.

Herriot, who cannot speak a word of either Lithuanian or Russian, but who is chairperson of the Darrowby Parent-Teacher Association, bursts into a school dressed in his work clothes and is fortunate that, thanks to the presence of an English teacher who is delighted with her first opportunity to actually speak to a real-life Englishman, he is not carried off by the police, as he would have been most anywhere in the world. Herriot's portrayed naïveté seems truly strained in these Baltic episodes.

A stormy voyage west is broken by a call in at the Polish port of Szczecin to load pigs. Herriot prefers to call the port by the old German name of Stettin. It is certainly easier for the monophonic narrator to pronounce. The voyage story is really not intrinsically interesting. However, the descriptions of the Danish crew and the Eastern Europeans provide opportunities for the author to exercise his skill at characterization, and these sketches give pleasure to the reader.

The briefer Turkish adventure is intrinsically more interesting and a better-crafted tale, employing dramatically a unity of action, direct continuity, suspense, humor, character frustration, relief, and a thought-provoking surprise resolution. The year is 1963, and Herriot is ready for another trip as a veterinary attendant. He is offered a trip to Istanbul with a cargo of Jersey cows, and he again jumps at the opportunity, once more apparently neglecting to discuss the assignment with Helen.

Herriot anticipates a leisurely seventeen-day Mediterranean cruise and a stay at a "five-star hotel" (*LGMTA,* 267). Things usually do not go well at first with Herriot. His innocent errors and bad luck, of course, are part of the characterization. It turns out that the journey is to be by plane, a huge worn out World War II Globemaster transport, one of the world's largest planes at the time. The elderly airplane, whose machinery continually breaks down, and whose tires are threadbare, is on its last leg—or should I say last engine? The crew, consisting of an English captain and two Americans, as well as of Herriot and the two farmers assigned to handle the cows, has an uneventful overnight flight to Munich for refueling. Then things begin to go wrong. Later that morning, over the Mediterranean, they discover that one engine is on fire. Nevertheless they reach Istanbul safely on three engines (*LGMTA*, 275).

Unloading is delayed because the hoist jams, and an electrician must be found to make repairs that take hours. Turkish agricultural officials pick and fuss as officials did in Klaipeda and Szczecin, but finally Herriot and his helpers, after almost twenty-four hours without anything to eat (the cows have had lots of quality hay), are ready for a wash, food, drink, and the promised luxury hotel. Instead they are informed by the captain that the inoperative engine cannot be repaired there and that the craft must be flown back to company headquarters in Copenhagen instead of to London. The Englishmen are stranded because the aircraft is considered unsafe. The export company must be phoned to get them transport home. To add to the growing disaster, the captain has been unable to find a hotel in Istanbul with vacancies because of a national holiday (*LGMTA*, 300).

The captain hires a minibus and they all set out to drive along the Bosporus looking for a place to stay. Herriot's descriptive powers are at his best: "As we sped through the teeming traffic on that gloriously sunny evening, exquisite mosques and minarets towered incongruously over modern tenements, then unexpectedly there would be a long stretch of waste ground with stubbly, scorched grass and garish billboards. Tremendous stone aqueducts, ancient and overgrown, appeared briefly in our windows, and were gone before I could do more than catch them on my film. The massive ruins of the walls of old Costantinople, the crumbling fortresses on the shattered walls—I glimpsed them briefly" (*LGMTA, 300–301*).

At last they find a decent accommodation, but Herriot must go to the local post office to call the London headquarters of the export company. The post office is a taxi ride away. He places the call only to learn that it will take an hour to make the connection, and he must taxi back to the hotel. He has still not eaten, and now he learns that all the rooms have been taken. Out of pity the management assigns him a "cell-like apartment in the basement." It contains only "a single un-made bed and a rumpled pile of blankets on a chair in the corner" (*LGMTA, 302*). Back up to the dining room for food at last, and raising a first forkful to his mouth, Herriot is called away by a taxi driver to the post office for his London call, but there, alas, the English woman at the company and Herriot cannot understand each other because the connection is so bad. He has failed his farmer friends, but they have saved him a tray of food.

The surprisingly unsophisticated Herriot (after all he is an educated professional man in his mid-forties) tells his companions that he will lay out the cost of a flight to London by purchasing tickets with a personal check. Feeling secure, they go out on the town looking for a pub in an Islamic city. After frustrating stops, they wind up in a friendly place they think is a tavern, where they get drinks that turn out to be nonalcoholic, and, when they try to pay, the waiter refuses their money. Slowly they come to realize that they have crashed a wedding reception! (*LGMTA, 308*). However, they are treated with typical Turkish courtesy and hospitality and made welcome by the newlyweds.

At the airport, naturally, British European Airlines refuses his check. Foolishly, they beg the captain to take them with him to Copenhagen on the unsafe plane with only three engines working. The captain wisely wants them to go to the British Consul for aid, but finally he acquiesces, and, fortunately, they make it to Copenhagen and then on to London. The story ends shockingly and poignantly. After returning home from the quick but very eventful trip, Herriot experiences what most of us have at times: a wondering if the experience actually happened or was only a dream or a fantasy. But "It all came back to me in stark truth when I heard, many months later, that, soon after the Istanbul flight, the Globemaster had plunged into the Mediterranean with the loss of all her crew. The news came to me indirectly, and I did my best to find out if it was true, but it was a long time afterwards and I had no success. Ever since, I have thought often about those men . . . and even now I still cling to the faint hope that terrible news was wrong" (*LGMTA*, 342). Herriot was touched, on the unconscious level, by the comradeship of humanity in danger, the fragility of mortality, and the fact that he had one weekend unwisely made himself hostage to Death.

The primary subject of *The Lord God Made Them All* is the archetypal flow of family and community life that metonymically supports the key contiguity in the Herriot saga: the concept that nature is all one cloth. The emotion that stirs the concept is love. Herriot does not use the word *love* often. One must infer its presence. Simply put, love for Herriot is the full and true caring for others; indeed, it is also the need to do so. The persona embraces the world from earth to sky, from breath to stone. This thematic love is a goal, achievable for a persona in a text, but an ideal for a real person.

The character of Helen recedes somewhat into the background as Herriot's familial interests focus on his children James (Jimmy) and Rosemary (Rosie). Helen's one moment of foregrounding in the book occurs when Herriot describes her 1947 confinement, when daughter Rosemary is born. The same midwife who delivered Jimmy, when Herriot was in the RAF, delivers Rosemary. This time Herriot is careful not to offend Nurse Brown, and although he is shocked that the infant's face is "all squashed and red and bloated, " he exclaims: "Gorgeous, really gorgeous" (*LGMTA*, 156). The climax of the birthing episode is Herriot's proud statement: "She is now Dr. Rosie in our community" (*LGMTA*, 157).

Jimmy gets the most family attention as he undergoes the rites of boyhood. His father is a role model. The child enjoys making rounds with the veterinarian and helping him by attending to gates and fetching equipment from the car. Stereotypically the boy, Jimmy gets into trouble. While Herriot is attending a patient, Jimmy climbs the wisteria outside the surgery window. Seeing his son in danger, the veterinarian does not know where to look first: to his patient or to his endangered child. The fall, as always, is inevitable. Jimmy is unhurt but must be chastised and cautioned. The worst possible penalties for him are the loss of the privilege of accompanying his father, and the loss of the miniature farmer's boots he had coveted and been given by Helen. As a little man he has bonded with his father through work, and he has also bonded with both the sturdy farmers he admires and the beasts they tend. His tiny boots tread a land he too grows to love. At the end of the "falling" episode, Herriot informs the reader that "this morsel of humanity . . . was later to become a far better veterinary surgeon than I could ever be, in fact, to quote thirty years later a dry Scottish colleague who had been through college with me and didn't mince words, 'A helluva improvement on his old man' "(*LGMTA*, 48).

Jimmy is the subject and the focus of several episodes, but the one all parents can relate to centers on the boy's piano solo in front of his music teacher, Miss Livingstone, his fellow students, his parents, and all the other parents at the Methodist Hall recital. Helen and James suffer the torment of the damned as they witness their child's inability to get through his piece despite repeated starts. Jimmy has to leave the piano. Herriot is sure the child is crushed with failure and shame. But Miss Livingstone is a wise teacher. At the end of the recital she gives Jimmy the chance for one more try. The intrepid and confident boy shouts: "Aye, aye, I'll have a go!" (*LGMTA,* 281). He succeeds at last.

Herriot, like many a master of an art or a craft, is a teacher too. The lesson for the pupil is perseverance; for the teacher, patience. One is always learning the craft he or she practices. The Herriot way is empirical, he teaches with the exemplum to push for practical experience. In a interview, the author shows the technique: "I can remember Donald [Sinclair] telling me one day, 'Alf, there is more t' be learned up a cow's arse than in many an encyclopaedia.' "[2] When Herriot is set up by a boastful student assistant and has to perform a bovine cesarean for the first time, he learns and teaches caution and the necessity of an individual's assuming personal responsibility for his or her actions (*LGMTA,* 63–75).

In this jumble book Rosemary is introduced most off-handedly, merely mentioned when on the cattle-boat bridge Herriot makes a radio-phone call and talks "to Helen and daughter Rosie in the darkness" (*LGMTA,* 108). Late in the text Rosie picks up where Jimmy, now in school, has had to leave off: accompanying and "assisting" Herriot on his rounds. Rosie, like Jimmy and his father, is musical. She sings to James as they drive through the countryside. Naturally, she assumes Jimmy's old responsibility for opening and closing the innumerable gates so Herriot can drive up to the farms without constantly getting in and out of his car. "Daddy," the three-year-old wonders, "how are you going to manage when I'm at school? All those gates to open and having to get everything out of the boot [trunk] by yourself. It's going to be awful for you" (*LGMTA,* 209).

The patriarchal Herriot purposely sets out to discourage his daughter from her career dream, to be a veterinarian with a large-animal country practice, like her father's practice, which Jimmy will qualify for and inherit. Herriot realizes that it is natural for his children, having grown up in a veterinary practice, to want a career like their father's. "There was no prob-

lem with Jimmy. He was a tough little fellow and well able
to stand the buffets of our job, but somehow I couldn't bear
the idea of my daughter being kicked and trodden on and
knocked down and covered with muck" (*LGMTA*, 209).
Writing in 1980 the author has his narrator apologize for his
actions. "I have never been a heavy father and have always
believed that children should follow their own inclinations.
But as Rosie entered her teens, I dropped a long series of broad
hints and perhaps played unfairly. . . . She finally decided to
be a doctor to humans. Now when I see the high percentage
of girls in the veterinary schools and observe the excellent
work done by the two girl assistants in our own practice, I
sometimes wonder if I did the right thing" (*LGMTA*, 210).

We learn that Siegfried has married and so has Tristan.
Siegfried moves out of Skeldale House to a residence outside
Darrowby, so James, Helen, and Jimmy have the run of the
house (*LGMTA*, 29). Captain Tristan Farnon of the Royal
Army Veterinary Corps has left the military and joined James's
nemesis, the Ministry of Agriculture. In one of life's and
literature's subtle ironies, the ever randy youth serves as an
"infertility investigation officer" (*LGMTA*, 30). Interestingly,
although in the previous volumes we had been introduced to
several of Siegfried's and Tristan's inamoratas, Herriot never
mentions the names of his friends' wives.

Naturally, the irrepressible Siegfried is featured in several
episodes. In their bachelor days together, the three young
goats competed for the favors of the attractive females of the
neighborhood. The beautiful if somewhat eccentric Miss
Grantley, desired by the comrades three, is a lover of goats,
the four-legged variety, who indicates her preference among
male veterinarians by sending the chosen one a test sample of
goat manure. "In ancient days the feudal knights would carry
a glove at their saddle bow or a scarf on their lance point as a
symbol of their lady's esteem, but with Miss Grantley, it was
goat droppings" (*LGMTA*, 94). Siegfried's sexual dominance
of the pack of three is indicated by Herriot:

If sheer male attractiveness entered into this situation, there was no doubt that Siegfried was out in front by a street. Tristan pursued the local girls enthusiastically and with considerable success; I had no reason to complain about my share of female company but Siegfried was in a different class. He seemed to drive women mad.

He didn't have to chase them; they chased him. I hadn't known him long before I realised that the tales I had heard about the irresistible appeal of tall, lean-faced men were true. And when you added his natural charm and commanding personality, it was inevitable that the goat droppings would land regularly by his plate (LGMTA, 94–95).

Readers of the Herriot memoirs who are also addicted viewers of the BBC's *All Creatures Great and Small* TV series must make a complete readjustment between the printed text and the visual portrayal when it comes to the characterization of Siegfried. In the pre-World War II episodes in any of the memoirs, Siegfried is under thirty, slim, and youthfully handsome. The inimitable Robert Hardy is seen on the small screen as a portly man in his late forties who needs bifocals to read. Peter Davison's excellent Tristan seems to be the right age for a son of Siegfried rather than a brother. The relationship between Siegfried and Tristan surely is played more as controlling father and passively resisting son in the series than in the books.

But Tristan in the texts is ever the Hermes figure, clever, persistent, fun loving, joke playing, devious, scheming, and subversive. Although perhaps less attractive and without the patriarchal power of his older brother, he has the traditional wile of the younger sibling, who must use brains to defeat his stronger older sibling, and thus Tristan can compete with occasional success. Finally, in the competition for Miss Grantley, he cleverly immerses himself in goat lore, wins the affection of the girl, and is rewarded with the droppings (*LGMTA,* 100). Droppings by the plate and droppings as a sign of sexual favor is so delightfully Herriot: scatological humor that is funny to the reader, and simultaneously a veterinarian's in-joke on the reader, meant to turn his or her stomach a bit.

Tristan's main entry in *The Lord God Made Them All* is again as a Loki, the archetypal Norse troublemaker. When James phones Tristan to announce the birth of Helen's and his daughter Rosemary, Tristan responds: "We've got to wet this baby's head, Jim" (*LGMTA*, 157). There is to be a surrogate baptism in beer, and a ritual of male bonding as Helen lies in her bed recovering from her labor earlier that day. James is eager for the excuse for heavy drinking: "I was ready for anything. 'Of course, of course, when are you coming over?' " he replies to Tristan.

Four male friends drink long into the night in the Black Horse pub. When closing hour comes they talk the landlord into breaking the law and letting them continue the Yorkshire bacchanal. He takes them into the cellar to drink among the barrels and crates. When Police Constable Goole arrives on the scene to make arrests, he is subverted into getting violently drunk. Herriot finally goes home having spent a great deal of the money needed for family expenses. The "maleness" of this experience is even to be shared by the child Jimmy, for when the inebriated James returns home he goes into his son's room, which was Tristan's room in the bachelor days, and looks down at his sleeping son, presumably breathing boozy fumes in the child's direction, and exults that with two children "I was becoming rich" (*LGMTA*, 165). Well, at least there are no more drunken episodes with Granville Bennett.

Food is even more of a pleasure for Herriot in *The Lord God Made Them All* than is alcohol. He describes with Dickensian deliciousness various meals, and he actually adores British cuisine! Consider the traditional Yorkshire Sunday dinner (served midday) of roast beef and Yorkshire pudding: "My wife had just dropped a slab of the pudding on my plate and was pouring gravy over it, a rich, brown flood with the soul of the meat in it and an aroma to dream of. . . . If I had some foreign gourmet to impress with the choicest sample of our British food, then this is what I would give him" (*LGMTA,* 6–7). Is Wight serious, or is this subtle satire?

One the happiest aspects of Herriot's working voyage on the Danish ship is the constant stream of excellent food directed toward him so that, the five-foot-ten-inch man learns the silent danger of cruising and is forced to do rigorous calisthenics to fight a growing bulge. A typical meal in the ship's mess consists of "exquisite asparagus soup in which floated meat balls and large stalks of asparagus. This was followed by what the captain describes as 'boneless birds'—tender veal steaks wrapped around strips of bacon, parsley and spices, with anchovies draped across them. We finished off with a sago pudding thickly sprinkled with cinnamon and with peaches nesting on its bosom. As I sipped my coffee and nibbled delicious Danish cheese, I felt I might have been eating at the Ritz" (*LGMTA,* 59). The fine, affectionate, mouth-watering description indicates a degree of sensual pleasure that borders on adoration, especially such images as "peaches nesting on its bosom."

At another meal there are "mountains of roast chicken with a piquant stuffing . . . surrounded by layers of cucumber done up with sugar and vinegar. Fruit followed, and of course, there was the ever-present array of herring in tomato, salami, salt beef, pork, smoked ham, bacon and endless kinds of Danish sliced sausages and cheese (*LGMTA,* 60–61). Other meals and delicacies are also passionately described.

H erriot takes pains in *The Lord God Made Them All* to show the reader how well-read he is. In repartee with his well-educated assistant Norman Beaumont, Herriot proves that he can hold his own in bantering quotes from Shakespeare and eighteenth- and nineteenth-century writers (*LGMTA,* 76). He later points out in a humorous story that George Bernard Shaw is one of his "heroes." However, talking about the playwright to his farmer clients is a mistake, for they have not heard of Shaw and cannot understand why the veterinarian is speaking familiarly about someone living in London (*LGMTA*, 211–15). The episode seems as much designed to demonstrate Herriot's cultural awareness as to present a mildly humorous episode.

Old characters and new enliven *The Lord God Made Them All*. Mr. Biggins, as vacillating, taciturn, parsimonious, suspicious, and thickheaded as ever, returns but is bested by Siegfried and James at last when they trick him into accepting new medicine, and they save his cow from quack remedies and premature destruction (*LGMTA*, 181–91).

Mean and nasty Walt Barnett, supposedly the richest man in Darrowby, "whom Siegfried had mortally offended by charging him ten pounds for castrating a horse" (*LGMTA*, 286), returns in a good mystery episode, this time as a cat lover. When he cries over the loss of his pet, Herriot likes him for the first time (*LGMTA*, 291).

Herriot reintroduces the saintly Sister (nurse) Rose, who, besides her full-time job taking care of humans, runs a dog sanctuary behind her house. The nurse and the veterinarian join forces whenever possible to save the lives of abandoned dogs (*LGMTA*, 132–42). Police Constable Goole, referred to earlier, is brought low because of his soft heart under a tough, official hide; his weakness for drink; and Tristan's machinations. He is yet another richly portrayed Herriot character (*LGMTA*, 161–65).

Veterinarian argot serves again as an architectonic in *The Lord God Made Them All*. The anatomy lesson includes nematodes (roundworms), the scapula (shoulder bone), supraspinatus and infraspinatus muscles, the radius (forearm bone), the ulna (inner forearm bone), and the tibia (includes the shin bone).

Animal troubles include hog cholera, chronic pleurisy, blackhead (turkey disease), listeriosis (parasitic infection), radial paralysis, demyelination of the brain (attack on nerve sheaths), endometritis (uterus-lining inflammation), actinobacillosis (wooden tongue), staphylococci, *demodex canis* (dog mites), sarcoptic mange (mite itch), demodectic mange, apnea (stopped breathing), bone spicule (sliver), helminthiasis (intestinal worms), coccidiosis (spore fever), hypertrophy (enlargement) of the rumenal walls, eclampsia (toxic pregnancy), and dyspnea (difficult breathing).

Treatments, procedures, and instruments include the fearsome-sounding Burdizzo bloodless castrator, crystal violet vaccine (for hog cholera), Stovarsol tablets (for sick turkeys), penicillin-streptomycin suspension, Terramycin (trademark for oxytetracycline), lugol's iodine (for infertility), catheters, nystagmus (involuntary side-to-side eye movement), fowler's solution of arsenic, odylen (for mites), potassium hydroxide (for slides), Pentothal (trademark for thiopental, anesthetic), Predsolan (early brand of cortisone), anthelmintics (worm killers), écraseur (wire loop for excisions), Universal Cattle Medicine, red blister, electuaries (sweetened medicines), the text *Udall's Practice of Veterinary Medicine,* and the ever effective *vis medicatrix naturae.*

Herriot's self-effacing gentility and compassion endure. When his old friend Andrew Bruce, a bowler-hatted banker, whom he had not seen since school days, comes to visit him, Herriot professes his awe of those who are good with figures and declares: "I have always had to use my fingers for counting" (*LGMTA,* 315). Herriot may not have had much experience counting money, but by 1980 Wight would have had quite a few opportunities to practice adding up considerable royalties.

Having to give a fatal overdose of anesthetic to Sister Rose's loveable, but incurably ill and suffering dog, Amber, deeply pains James even though he knows the that the procedure is "an easy way out from that prison which would soon become a torture chamber" (*LGMTA,* 141). But although he was at least able to save Amber, whom he truly cared for, from "the ultimate miseries: the internal abscesses and septicaemia that await a dog suffering from a progressive and incurable demodectic mange" (*LGMTA,* 141), the healer was overpowered by a sense of loss and failure, and to this day he is haunted by the death. Often "the picture of Amber comes back into my mind. It is always dark, and she is always in the headlight's beam" (*LGMTA,* 142). Herriot has connected with an almost universal human emotional experience. Any pet owner who has lost a beloved little companion knows and shares Herriot's sadness.

In another case, Herriot is happy when a patient's master is determined to keep various of his animals alive despite the grave prognoses of the veterinarian. Farmer Jack Scott may not understand the diagnosis, but he refuses to give up hope for any beast. He prays for his animals, and Herriot is reminded of a line from Coleridge: "He prayeth best who loveth best all things both great and small" (*LGMTA,* 250). Farmer Scott loves and respects life. His animals survive, make do, and are happy with what functions survive their ailments. The farmer is imbued with the life force, and his animals remind Herriot that medicine is not an exact science, while they teach the reader that life is precious and worth living even when handicaps are great.

Herriot knows and advocates the value of pets in therapy. Ron Cundall, a former miner who had been crushed and broken by a collapsing roof, is bed-ridden, but he is sustained by the love of and for his dog: "The little feller's made all the difference. You're never alone when you've got a dog" (*LGMTA,* 227).

Herriot ends *The Lord God Made Them All* with a confusing chapter that bounces back and forth between 1955 and the time of the completion of the writing of the book, 1981. He states that now Helen and he are "about to celebrate our Ruby

Wedding" anniversary (*LGMTA*, 370). He remembers a time in the 1950s when Siegfried and he were nostalgically reminiscing in the garden of Skeldale House about the time in 1938 depicted in *All Creatures Great and Small* in which James came to Darrowby looking for a job. They have enjoyed their personal and professional lives. They know then (1950s) that they are in "the high noon of country practice" (*LGMTA*, 372). They have wives and children whom they love and enjoy. They have seen a revolution in their profession with the coming of antibiotics. Siegfried's eyes shine with enthusiasm when he says: "I tell you, this, James. There are great days ahead!" (*LGMTA*, 373).

Wight seems to be bringing the Herriot saga to a close, one that would of course prove to be temporary. *The Lord God Made Them All* creates the impression that the primary and central material, his experiences in veterinary practice during the earlier years of his professional life, has been mined to exhaustion. This depletion explains the need for all the tying up and concluding at the end of *The Lord God Made Them All*. The confused chronology and the direct reliance on journal entries indicate a tiring author. It will be more than ten years before the memoirs will be resumed.

Despite the book's narrative shortcomings, it provides much insight and many pages of sheer pleasure. Henrietta Buckmaster sums up *The Lord God Made Them All* quite well: "Herriot has so enlarged our understanding of animals that the debt is considerable even when the book is less than one might hope."[3]

7

Every Living Thing

When *Every Living Thing* was published in 1992, the book immediately jumped on to the *New York Times* best-seller list and remained there for well over thirty weeks. The subsequent paperback edition performed similarly on the paperback list. Clearly, the Herriot public had been hungry for another memoir. During the eleven years between texts, this hunger was fed by the presentation and continued rerunning on the BBC in Britain and on PBS in America of the seven television series. The public was not disappointed. Perhaps written under the pressure of fans and editors crying out for more of the same, *Every Living Thing* reopens the Herriot saga, provides fifty-two chapters and 342 pages of pleasure, continues the story of the Herriot family and ensemble, introduces new characters, and delivers a package of timeless anecdotes of Herriot's interaction with the people of Yorkshire and their animals.

With his four previous titles, Wight ran out of lines from Cecil Frances Alexander's verse, and so he turned to the Bible for his next title, choosing to symbolize his inherently deep conviction that humans not only were given dominion, or obtained it, over other life on earth but that dominion came with the codicils of responsibility and compassion. In the latter respect all of the Herriot saga illustrates an amendment to the dictum of chapter 1, verse 28 of Genesis, which is featured as a headnote to the text: "Be fruitful and multiply, and replenish the earth and subdue it: and have dominion over the fish of the sea and over the fowl of the air, and over every living thing that moveth upon the earth." Herriot's text demonstrates that with dominion comes care.

Once again the framing structure of the text is complicated and sometimes confusing, but essentially the configuration is as follows: Herriot is speaking to his audience in 1991 about events in the 1950s in which he frequently reminisces about incidents in his pre-RAF days. A few of these events were mentioned in the early texts, and he uses them as refreshers, reminders, and linking devices.

In the now formulaic way, the memoir begins with a powerfully symbolic story within the major Herriot theme of near death and resurrection, a well-crafted episode that is a microcosmic introduction to the full text and which sets the tone of the entire work. The time is "in the fifties" on a very cold Yorkshire March morning. Herriot and Farmer Kettlewell are standing in a "cobbled farmyard watching a beautiful horse dying because of my incompetence."[1] The narrator's perspective is from the present, for he is nostalgic about the disappearance of the draft horse through replacement with the tractor. But at the time of the story some of the workhorses, like "the magnificent Shire" he thinks he has killed, are still in use. Herriot has unwisely administered two medications for the horse's allergic condition he is treating with antihistamines, and the beast has collapsed and appears to be seconds from death.

The two stunned and forlorn men stand over the huge animal, and Herriot thinks: "What was I going to say? I'm terribly sorry, Mr. Kettlewell, I just can't understand how this happened. My mouth opened, but nothing came out, not even a croak. And, as though looking at a picture from the outside, I became aware of the square of farm buildings with the dark, snow-streaked fells rising behind under a lowering sky, of the biting wind, the farmer and myself, and the motionless body of the horse" (*ELT,* 4).

Almost miraculously, and luckily for Herriot, the horse gets over its reaction and suddenly rises. The farmer is ignorant of what has occurred medically and thinks the horse's reaction is what was to be expected in the treatment. Of course he was frightened, but all he can say to his veterinarian is: "Aye, well, it's wonderful new treatment. But I'll tell tha summat. . . . I hope you don' mind me sayin' this but . . . ah think it's just a bit drastic" (*ELT,* 4). The episode is dramatic; indeed, craftedly melodramatic. It contains danger to a beautiful and valuable living thing, sharply drawn characters, tension, suspense, surprise, and a happy ending with a humorous punch. Finally, Herriot, in his seventies, laughs at himself in his thirties, and then describes a patch of the grand Yorkshire scenery to remind us, as he is wont to do, how happy he was and is to live where he does.

> I drove away from the farm and pulled up my car in the lee of a dry-stone wall. A great weariness had descended upon me. This sort of thing wasn't good for me. I was getting on in years now [only in his thirties]—and I couldn't stand these shocks like I used to. . . . The feeling of guilt and bewilderment persisted, and with it the recurring thought that there must be easier ways of earning a living than as a country veterinary surgeon. . . . I leaned back and closed my eyes. When I opened them a few minutes later, the sun had broken through the clouds, bringing the green hillsides and the sparkling ridges of snow to vivid life, painting the rocky outcrops with gold. I wound the window down and breathed in the cold, clear air, drifting snow, fresh and tangy from the moorland high above. A curlew cried, breaking the enveloping silence, and on the grassy bank by the roadside I saw the first primroses of spring (*ELT,* 4–5).

Nature has rejuvenated him again. Peace comes. His doubt about his professional competence fades. As he drives away he realizes again how good a life he has among the hardworking people of North Yorkshire and their animals in "this thrilling countryside." He knows he "was lucky to be a vet in the Yorkshire Dales" (*ELT,* 5). To put it all precisely, chapter 1 is the essential Herriot; it has everything.

Wight, not surprisingly, is now completely at home with his format, and thus Herriot is more at ease too. He is not embarrassed to admit that he admires John Wayne. He salts the text with far fewer quotes from literary masters. He no longer feels that one can judge a man by the cut of his quotes, so to speak.

The iterative subjects of *Every Living Thing* are three: the story of the Herriot family in the 1950s and their search for the "perfect" home; the coming and the going of the fabulous animal-loving, Scottish-born and Yorkshire-bred assistant (reverse of Herriot), Calum Buchanan; and Herriot's valiant struggle to be accepted by the family cats.

At the opening of the 1950s' chord, the first iterative subject, the Herriots are still living in and have the full run of Skeldale House, which Siegfried has vacated in order to live more comfortably with his wife in a house outside of Darrowby. Mrs. Hall's excellent service to the bachelor household is obviously not needed, and she simply disappears from the narrative. In the BBC TV series, she dies during the war, when all her young men are away in service.

Seeing Helen on her knees scrubbing the front-door steps of Skeldale House, a farmer says: "This house is a woman-killer Mr Herriot. . . . Aye, it's a grand old house, but it's a woman-killer" (*ELT,* 85). On hearing these words, with their slight indictment of Herriot's lack of chivalry and gentlemanly concern for his wife, the sensitive veterinarian immediately decides that somehow he will get Helen out of that house. For the patriarchal Herriot, the problem is that he views Helen as an obsessive-compulsive housewife yet at the same time he unconsciously encourages her to be one. On the surface he expresses concern. He gazes down at the kneeling woman and thinks: "This was crazy, and the words 'Please stop it!' bubbled up in my mind. But I didn't speak them. It was no good. I had tried to stop her again and again but it was a waste of time. That was the way she was made. She was domestically minded. . . . She was absolutely determined to keep inside and outside clean and tidy" (*ELT*, 86).

Herriot claims to be "worried and exasperated" that Helen is such a Victorian "Good Woman": "I was married to a beautiful, intelligent, warm-hearted woman, but I wished . . . that she would be kinder to herself and take more time to rest, and when we were first married tried by pleading and at times by making angry scenes, which I wasn't much good at, to make her alter her ways, but it was like talking to a wall—she slogged on regardless" (*ELT*, 86).

Herriot, however, loves food, and Helen is a great cook. "I had never met anybody who could work such magic with food, and as a dedicated eater I realised my good luck, but I wished fervently that she would spend less time over the oven" (*ELT*, 86). James sends Helen mixed and conflicting messages: don't work so hard cooking and cleaning, but I do love my food and am proud that my home is spotless.

In the end, the anguished veterinarian accepts her fastidiousness and is able to "console myself that I could hear her singing as she went round the house with her Hoover [vacuum cleaner] and duster" (*ELT*, 86). A thoughtful reader might wonders how Helen Herriot would "speak" these scenes if the author were Joan Wight. The old house, although fine for the practice, is too large, and, without central heating, too cold for a twentieth-century British family to reside in. Herriot notes that "the main casualty was Helen, who was plagued with terrible chilblains (swelling, burning, and reddening) round her ankles" (*ELT*, 87).

He jumps to 1990 and to their Golden Wedding anniversary, at which point he notes that Helen "still sings as she potters busily around in another, mercifully much smaller house. It dawned on me long ago that she's happy this way" (*ELT*, 86). The author has his narrator take very good care of their collective motility. Like many successful men of retirement age who have worked hard and achieved much, Herriot has time and inclination to look back and in retrospect valorizes his support system.

Regardless, Skeldale House must be abandoned. Herriot's early attempts to find more suitable housing for his family are nearly disastrous. First he covets a small, tidy house that is to be auctioned off for a widow. He looks around the kitchen and is positive he will get the house. "I could just see Helen at that [kitchen] window, looking out on the little garden" (*ELT*, 88). Apparently Herriot does not discuss his decision with Helen, but he does invite her to attend the auction with him. There the bidding quickly exceeds his maximum bank loan, but he continues to bid wildly despite Helen's desperate pleading: "No Jim, no! We haven't any money!" (*ELT*, 89). Finally, Helen stops him, and the only good thing that results from the incident is that a poor widow receives much more money for her house than she has ever dreamed of getting (*ELT*, 90).

Herriot falls in love with another house to be auctioned. Again the bidding rages beyond their means, but Helen, "a big strong woman," keeps a firm grip on his hand ready to reduce Jim's "fingers to a pulp" if he attempts to shout the family into financial disaster.

Then a wife and husband architectural team convince Herriot that building his own house is the answer. This time Helen is more involved in the decision: "Helen nodded too" (*ELT*, 143). It is finally dawning on Herriot that marital relationships are economic partnerships too. For all of his appreciation of Helen's cooking, cleaning, nursing, childbearing and rearing, bookkeeping, telephone answering, scheduling, and secretaryship, Herriot had never seemed either to understand or be able to acknowledge her economic significance in what is after all a tony mom and pop business.

Herriot assumes the role of general contractor for the house. In addition to his practice he must coordinate the joiners, bricklayers, and electricians, not an easy job in post–World War II Britain. I recall, when residing in York in the 1960s, the painfully slow construction of a tiny "super" market at the end of my street. Every time the derby-(bowler-) hatted boss left the site, the workers took out a soccer ball and kicked it around the road until someone spotted the boss returning. The small project took a year.

Herriot's bad luck holds true. Just before the roof is scheduled to go on, a ninety-mile-per-hour gale blows the whole unsupported edifice down (*ELT,* 146). Herriot accepts the blow philosophically, and the house is rebuilt and completed. Rowan Garth is the name of the new house. It is "modern, reasonably small, convenient . . . and warm" (*ELT,* 154).

The only problem is that the children are physically nearer, and very much into pop music, which they blast out from record player and radio. Herriot has difficulty handling this aspect of the generation gap, especially coming as he does from a classical music background. But eventually he gets used to rock and to Elvis. What begins as "loud, unpleasant noise" turns into identifiable songs, like "Blue Suede Shoes," "Don't Be Cruel," and "Jailhouse Rock," of which Herriot actually grows fond, so that thirty years later, he says of Presley's music: "any of his songs coming over the radio can transport me back to those mornings in the kitchen at Rowan Garth with the children at their cornflakes, my dog at my side and whole world young and carefree" (*ELT,* 155).

In *The Lord God Made Them All,* Grandma Clarke, when learning that Jimmy was then ten and Rosie six during the time spent at Rowan Garth, says to Herriot: "Maybe you don't know it, Mr. Herriot, but this is the best time of your life" (369). Herriot, like most parents, comes to learn that truth afterward, when the home is quiet. Interestingly, it is when talking nostalgically of the youth of his children that Herriot makes one of the very few references to his own parents, noting that his family did "visit my parents in Glasgow" (*ELT,* 154).

The Herriots, however, spend only a year at Rowan Garth.

They are tempted by Siegfried to buy a residence called High Field House, in a tiny village of a dozen houses a few miles from Darrowby, but in the heart of the practice, where they can truly live "on the edge of the wild" (*ELT,* 269). This happiest of Herriot homes is the last until ostensibly they move to a much smaller, more manageable domicile after the children are grown and have left home. This dénouement is quietly mentioned earlier in the memoir (*ELT,* 86) and noted here earlier. As *Every Living Thing* is mainly concerned with events in the 1950s when the children grow into their teens, it is not surprising that a primary structuring subject is the basic act of nest building: making a home, nurturing children, loving pets. As at least one other critic has noted, the sheer simplicity and accessible ordinariness is so charming, sentimental, and seemingly uncontrived that it is nearly impossible not to love Herriot's world.[2]

The second iterative narrative, the one most central to *Every Living Thing,* is the coming, the two years in residence as veterinary assistant, and the going of Calum Buchanan, the "vet with the badger," to whom five chapters are devoted. Herriot fans of both the memoirs and the TV productions will realize, upon reading *Every Living Thing,* that the eighteen Calum episodes in the TV series four, five, six, and seven of the show *All Creatures Great and Small* were taken from unpublished Herriot manuscripts[3] and only appeared in print long after the entire television production was completed and aired. Calum's relations with the beautiful housekeeper Molly and with the lovely Emma, the daughter of Siegfried's veterinary friend, are not in *Every Living Thing,* where Calum is true from first to last to his bride-to-be, Dierdre.

Calum assumes a composite role in *Every Living Thing,* incorporating Tristan's fun-loving, ingratiating personality, Siegfried's eccentricity, and James's courting persona. He is also, as Tristan was, the attractive young tyro. Calum succeeds the assistant John Crooks, who was introduced in *The Lord God Made Them All* (34) as the later provider of Herriot's overseas assignments. Calum spends two years in the practice and has a profound affect on Herriot and on the community. He is an obsessive animal lover. He alights from his train in Darrowby with his pet badger, Marilyn, on his shoulder, and in the course of his stay in Skeldale House, his personal menagerie grows, to Siegfried's ever increasing frustration and chagrin, to include three badgers, an owl, unnumbered fox cubs, several dogs, a pair of Dobermans (one pregnant), a friend's monkey, and "a couple of rabbits and a hare" (*ELT*, 249). But Calum is both an endearing person and an outstanding veterinary surgeon, whom the customers soon prefer.

He has come directly from school, and his information and techniques are fresh. Perhaps his most significant contribution to the practice and to James personally is that he encourages his employer to do surgery he had previously been reluctant to attempt "from a lack of confidence" and thus to increase the revenue of the practice (*ELT*, 150). He also makes James aware of the realities of the future for the practice: "Calum raised a finger. 'Well, with respect, Jim, you've got to change your ideas. Small-animal work is the thing of the future and the day has gone when country vets can turn their backs on routine things like spays just because they think they haven't the time' " (*ELT*, 150).

Calum becomes engaged to Dierdre, and the paternalistic or avuncular James approves of her: "She was quite tall, and the first words that came to me were 'kind' and 'motherly.' But I would like to banish any thought that being kind and motherly meant that she wasn't attractive. Dierdre was very attractive indeed and now, nearly forty years later, when I think of her wonderful family of six young Buchanans I feel I deserve full marks for intuition" (*ELT*, 245).

Calum takes Dierdre to live in another small North Yorkshire town while he continues his assistant's work, until, to James's shock, he accepts a position in Nova Scotia (*ELT*, 331). Herriot genuinely cares for and professionally admires his eccentric, nature-fixated protégé. Like Tristan, whose presence now in the extended narrative has receded, Calum represents characteristics that Herriot admires but cannot emulate because they are simply not compatible with his conservatism and deep need to conform, fit in, and be accepted as a respectable member of the community. Calum stands for intrepid independence, freedom of action, carefreeness, indifference to appearances, and a love of adventure.

Twenty years after Buchanan leaves Yorkshire, Herriot learns that his friend is in Papua New Guinea (*ELT*, 333). Letters come from exotic addresses as Dierdre and Calum successfully adjust to life in a near Stone Age culture. Herriot learns in 1988 from one of the Buchanans's daughters that Calum the compulsive collector of birds and beasts now has "11 Border collies, 2 pig dogs (Labrador crosses), 2 water buffalo, 5 horses, many cattle, sheep, goats, an assortment of chickens, ducks, guinea fowl and a huge flock of homing pigeons" (*ELT*, 334). Herriot seems a little envious. Buchanan has led a life that one part of Herriot's psyche would like to have tried.

The third iterative, structuring sequence in *Every Living Thing* is Herriot's struggle, at High Field House, to win the trust and affection of Ginny and Olly, the wild feline brother and sister whose mother brought then near to the house, saw them fed by Helen, and left them or was killed (*ELT*, 274). Helen feeds and tries to care for the cats, although the animals remain outdoors in all weather. They share affection with Helen, recognizing her great maternal instinct, but distrust the veterinarian despite the fact that he is a cat lover and is proud of his "feline bedside manner" (*ELT*, 290). Their distrust results from his occasionally rounding them up for spaying or treatment. James is hurt, mortified, and frustrated by their distrust of him. He loves animals. Caring compassionately is his life's work, and when he must inflict some pain in the way of treatment, it is only for the animal's benefit. But, of course, they cannot understand that. A great unspoken wish in Herriot is that he, who speaks so eloquently for "animals who have no voice to tell us their woes,"[4] cannot explain to them that he is trying to succor them. Sometimes Herriot's patients seem to comprehend his gentleness, caring, and compassion, but he can never be sure that his perception of that comprehension is not a projection of his desire.

It is Helen who, after years with the cats have passed, teaches the animal doctor how to win the confidence of the cats. She, as a woman, a mother, and a homemaker, has more control of her time. His life is "one long rush." She feeds the animals, talks to them, pets them "day in, day out" (*ELT*, 338). The lesson for Herriot and us all is patience. Securing love and confidence takes commitment and time. Affection is a plant that grows, not an instant purchase. Herriot takes up the food and milk and begins "one of the little sagas of my life" (*ELT*, 338), the winning of Ginny and Olly. He perseveres and finally feels triumphant one day as the ever suspicious Olly allows James to stroke his fur. But Herriot's triumph soon turns bitter. Fort-eight hours later Olly is dead of strychnine poisoning (*ELT*, 339). We learn that a veterinarian is no different from other people when a beloved pet dies. However, Herriot tales are about hope and redemption, not despair, and so applying Helen's caring, time-consuming procedures, he wins Ginny's affection too.

With the passing of time and the maturing of the children, Helen grows in stature, takes more control of her own life, and receives some of the kind of attention she was given by the courting narrator in *All Creatures Great And Small*. She has a more proactive and central role in *Every Living Thing* compared to her limited, retroactive presence in *The Lord God Made Them All*.

Once more, as in *The Lord God Made Them All*, Herriot cries mea culpa over his successful scheme to keep his daughter Rosemary from considering a career in veterinary medicine.

He says: "Maybe I was wrong" (*ELT,* 49). His excuse is that "it is all so different now. We have long plastic gloves to protect us when we are doing smelly jobs" (*ELT,* 49), and in several places in the text he points out that small animal work expanded far beyond expectations to become more than half of the practice. Herriot could not bear to think that the girl he had feminized would do the physically hard, dirty large animal work (*ELT,* 50). What Herriot, even in 1992, cannot comprehend is that women are able to, and are currently doing, the job of treating farm animals as well as other work requiring strength, endurance, and courage in such obvious fields as nursing, construction, the military, police work, and fire fighting.

But although I have taken pains in my criticism of the five Herriot memoirs to indicate the deeply embedded patriarchal elements in the narrator's character, I must in fairness also point out that Herriot does have many fine, redeeming traits that feminists and contemporary women in general can only admire: he never disparages marriage, but supports it whole-heartedly; he married young and devoted his professional and personal life to the support of his family; he remains faithful to his marriage vows; he is a loving, caring husband and father; he respects women of all ages and classes; he appreciates and has high regard for woman's nurturing nature; he can see beauty in women of all ages; he is nonviolent, and, although a rabid football (soccer) fan, he is never in nor condones fist-fights. He does not take male aggression lightly, never, for instance, assuming that in cases of physical aggression "boys will be boys," and he pointedly despises all bullies.

Herriot is as good as his word. As a bachelor he treated women with respect and courted them like a gentleman. Women were not numbered prizes for him. He does not transgress against women. He does not take arrogant stands on so-called male prerogatives. He views Tristan's randiness and often frustrated attempts at promiscuity as adolescent and amusing. Finally, and perhaps most significantly, as the saga progresses and as the narrator ages, Herriot learns to question and liberalize early, inbred patriarchal values.

Perhaps because author and narrator are aging, Herriot dwells on personal illness for the first time in the memoirs. We learn that earlier in his career, in the 1950s, he fell ill with a common farmer's and veterinarian's disease contracted from handling diseased animals: brucellosis. Herriot reports that many veterinarians have had their health ruined by the disease (*ELT,* 62). Years later Herriot endures recurring attacks of fever that seem temporarily to affect his psychological balance so that he reacts to the infection by appearing somewhat intoxicated, a condition that causes great amusement in his children.

Of course Herriot must make it funny too. Because he is semidelirious one day, he becomes involved in an incident that he fears will result in a charge of sexual harassment. Mrs. Featherstone, an overly protective and doting dog owner, who continually brings healthy Rollo to the surgery, and whom James usually fobs off with a harmless placebo for the animal, arrives when the veterinarian is suffering from one of his attacks. Because she says it is urgent, he gets out of bed to attend the patient. He notices for the first time that "she wasn't a bad-looking woman! Very, very nice, in fact" (*ELT,* 66). He thinks that what he should do with the wealthy, imperious pet-hypochondriac is "grab her, give her a big, smacking kiss and a good long squeeze and all our past misunderstandings would melt away like the morning mist in the sun" (*ELT,* 65–66). Instead he finds himself laughing at her uncontrollably, and while insisting that there is nothing wrong with Rollo, he tries to poke her in the ribs with his finger. Fortunately, Mrs. Featherstone evades the maneuver and stares unbelievingly at Herriot, saying: "You can't really mean all this!" The reeling Herriot assures her that he indeed does (*ELT,* 68). The dazed woman leaves.

Next morning Herriot, coming out of his feverish state, is shocked as he tries to recall what he has done to the woman. Did he possibly paw at her?

> Had I really attempted to embrace her? Had I given her a little cuddle as I walked her down the passage? . . . Of one thing I could be sure—I had been guilty of the most ghastly impropriety and I had a searing conviction that I would have to pay dearly for it. Certainly she would never set foot in my surgery again. The whole shameful story would get around. She might even report me to the Royal college. I could see the headline in the *Darrowby and Houlton Times* VETERINARY SURGEON ON SERIOUS CHARGE, HERRIOT TO APPEAR BEFORE DISCIPLINARY BODY (*ELT,* 68–69).

He sets off for a stroll around town and to his horror sees Mrs. Featherstone heading for him. He thinks he is about to receive hell, but it is the 1950s, and the woman has seen the error of her foolish ways. Rather than accusing him of misbehaving, she exclaims: "Really, Mr. Herriot, you did me a service last night" (*ELT,* 69). She has learned not to waste a man's time with her unreasonable concern for her dog. She is going to be a sensible pet owner from now on. However, writing in 1992, Herriot implies that the incident could have been a professional and personal disaster if it happened now. When he thinks of the evening of the occurrence "I still get an attack of shivers" (*ELT,* 70).

Later in the text Herriot's illness prevents him on another occasion from making rounds alone, and he must go out in the company of Calum. Several times Herriot makes reference to the various hazards of his trade. Herriot purposely works against the "romance" of animal medicine. He resists projection as a paradigm, implying that young people have to be made aware of the limitations and negativity of the practice of veterinary medicine.

Herriot's inferiority complex and insecurity, a manifestation of which has been noted earlier when Calum has to convince James that he can perform routine operations in the surgery, are presented again in a most interestingly symbolic way. Kind old white-headed Mrs. Pumphrey appears once more and does a 1990s politically correct deed by helping a new Chinese restaurant succeed by giving it her frequent patronage and having her chauffeur-driven limousine parked outside. Tricky Woo had been depressed because he is, after all, descended from a long line of Chinese emperors and cannot bear to hear his own people denigrated by the locals (*ELT*, 28). Tricky Woo is very old in the 1950s. We were introduced to him circa 1939, but at least he no longer goes "flop-bott" (*ELT*, 36).

Always very generous to James, Mrs. Pumphrey shows him her deceased husband's substantial wardrobe and offers him a superb suit of Lovat tweed tailored on Saville Row. Herriot gratefully accepts, but when he brings it home and tries it on, he despairs as it is far too large for him. James, small of stature, cannot fill the "rich" suit of the successful industrialist, Mr. Pumphrey. The prudent Helen insists on taking the garment to the tailor for alteration, and when it returns, the jacket is fine but the trouser waist is around his chest. But the jacket covers the waist and he looks incredibly fine. However, the suit is really too heavy for indoor use, and when he attends an important meeting in it he drips sweat and nearly collapses of heat prostration. Still, Herriot the outsider impresses the gentry in the "borrowed robes" of the upper class. While he is hiding in a toilet stall with the jacket off, he hears Sir Henry and Lord Darborough praise his support of a poor hill farmer as well as the fact that the young veterinarian "Knows his clothes. Splendid suit. Rather envy him his tailor" (*ELT*, 43).

What makes *Every Living Thing* the most enjoyable narrative since *All Creatures Great and Small* is the superb characterization. Herriot just gets better and better at the task. A veritable parade of living characters march through the text, some amusing, some sad, some humble, and some proud, like the nearby veterinarian Hugo Mottram whose "imperious blue eyes" regard James with distaste as he accuses the young veterinarian of being dishonest (*ELT,* 51). Herriot had envied the older veterinarian for his looks: "He was the perfect picture of my idea of a country vet; check cap, immaculate hacking jacket, knee breeches, stockings and brogues together with a commanding presence and hawk-like, handsome features" (*ELT,* 51).

Mottram falsely accuses James and Siegfried of raiding his clients. He is a hard, unbending, competitive, suspicious person with an acute, almost doglike sense of territoriality, and a sociopathic personality, or, in Siegfried's terms, "a snooty bugger" (*ELT,* 53). He has rejected Siegfried's generous and good-natured offer of hospitality. Events conspire to make him more antagonistic to the new, young practice, but Siegfried and James return scorn and anger with respect and unselfish service as they save the life of Mottram's favorite horse, with the result that Mottram changes attitude entirely, comes to apologize, is put at ease by the ever generous Siegfried, and the three men bond their new friendship over a bottle of malt whiskey (*ELT,* 61).

Again and again Herriot valorizes gentlemanliness, traditionally coded British behavior that requires respect for privacy, exquisite courtesy, socioempathy, and good manners. Some say it was and is declining. The upwardly mobile Herriot "has made loyalty and kindness the crowning virtues."[5] As an outsider who has come to English life, he naturally embraces this code, which in addition fits so well with his innate conservatism and class consciousness.

. . .

Sister Rose, radiologist and animal shelterer, returns from *The Lord God Made Them All* to match Rupe Nellist, a man "with a pronounced limp in his right leg, a relic of childhood polio" (*ELT,* 316), with Titch, an abandoned dog with an unset broken femur and able to walk only on three legs—Herriot always tries to symmetrize his world. Handicaps exist as aberrations in an otherwise perfect Deistic creation, but they can often be overcome. These handicaps include outsiderhood, otherness, and feelings of inferiority over shortness of stature or about background.

Wishing to help the dog, Herriot, thanks to Calum's urging and confidence building, goes deeper into orthopedic surgery than he has ever before attempted. The operation is a success, and eventually Titch runs on all four legs to the satisfaction of all including the narrator who in helping the little creature very much helped himself.

Mrs. Bartram, whose dog Pup is "an enormous, shaggy creature of doubtful ancestry and with a short temper" (*ELT,* 8), and who exists on fish and chips, is obviously working class: living in her kitchen chair, "fat, massive, deadpan, the invariable cigarette dangling from her lips" (*ELT,* 8). She is a stereotypical working-class woman with a working-class dog: both fat and indolent. Unconsciously, Herriot seems to be revealing his middle-class prejudice and fear of the class below when he says of mistress and dog: "as I looked at the two, they had a great similarity sitting there, bolt upright, facing each other. Both huge, immobile, but giving an impression of latent power" (*ELT,* 8). Clearly, Herriot does not want to get too close to either mistress or pet. Of course the clever veterinarian figures out a way to treat the dangerous patient: he prescribes "Tablets for dog. One to be given three times daily inserted in chips" (*ELT,* 12).

The confectioner Geoffrey Hatfield, with his "silver-haired, leonine head," is an aristocrat of merchants. It is a pleasure and a privilege to be served by this most dignified and courteous of merchants, but when his cat Alfred falls ill,

Mr. Hatfield's composure and demeanor waste away, endangering his position as a town institution and his very livelihood. A Herriot operation saves the cat, and to everyone's relief and pleasure, restores a measure of order, grace, and comity to the Yorkshire universe (*ELT,* 22). Nowhere in Herriot's narratives or in Wight's interviews does Charles Dickens come up as an inspiration for Herriot's characterizations, but slightly exaggerated and gently satirizing constructs like Mr. Hatfield appear to have a nineteenth-century ancestry.

Lord Hulton (sounds like Yorkshire's Castle Bolton) appears again to offer a few monosyllabic expletives like "Oh, crumbs" (*ELT,* 139). Mr. Bendelow, the garrulous tailor who never delivers on time, is guarded from disgruntled, desperately frustrated customers by his dog Blanco, a great beast who at the appropriate protective moment menacingly rises like "a surfacing white whale" (*ELT,* 132). Arnold Braithwaite appears to be the town liar, and he suffers much derision and scorn for his tales of comradeship with the notables of the British sports world. At the moment he seems destined for humilation before his neighbors at a men's hockey match between Yorkshire and Lancashire, but to the amazement of all doubters, the "sports greats" greet him with: "It's our old chum. . . . We've been looking for you everywhere" (*ELT,* 175).

Wearing a face mask and picked up in an alley by the Darrowby police, "The Cisco Kid" turns out to be poor, sister-vexed Bernard "Useless" Wain, who has forgotten to remove the handkerchief he uses to protect his delicate nose from the barnyard odors he must endure on his farm (*ELT,* 230–35). The farm hand Nat Briggs never forgives Herriot for accidentally inoculating his left buttock with a minuscule amount (if any) of a cow abortion drug (*ELT,* 263). He claims that Herriot has prevented him from having children, but his fellow workers, who are enjoying his predicament, tell the veterinarian: "Don't listen to 'im, Mr. Herriot. . . . He can't do it properly—he's only makin' excuses" (*ELT,* 265). Sometime later, to Herriot's chagrin, he jabs Briggs again. This time the hypodermic has an antibiotic in it. Of course Briggs is furious. Later, however, Herriot learns that "Nat's become a Dad!" (ELT, 266), twins in fact. The co-workers of course jocularly insist that since Nat "blamed you for stoppin' the job with that first injection you gave 'im. . . . Well the second jab must have been the antidote!" (ELT, 266).

And then there is Albert Budd, a great big man and a great big farter, whom Calum accidentally puts in an embarrassing social situation by establishing a Highland dancing club (ELT, 270). Herriot's humor is upon occasion wonderfully scatological as befits a person who earns his living with an arm often reaching deeply into the rear ends of great beasts. But all in all Herriot's human characters and anthropomorphized animals seem destined to live their fictive lives long, long after they and the places they inhabited are gone and forgotten.

Like all the memoirs *Every Living Thing* is informed and structured by the discourse of veterinary practice. In this text the use of professional argot and the number and scope of veterinary references are fewer than in any of the preceding texts, probably because both the author and the narratee construct are older, in retirement years, and less active professionally. The animal anatomy lessons end. Diseases and problems of animals discussed in the text include opisthotonos (body arching), feline viral rhinotracheitis (cat flu), eczema, conjunctiva, colic, mammary tumor, cerebrocortical necrosis (brain disease), brucellosis, necrotic cotyledons (diseased uterine surfaces), metritis (inflammation of the uterus), laminitis (hoof disease), and urticaria (allergic rash).

Treatments, drugs, and procedures include oxyter soluble powder (for cat flu), penicillin intramammary tubes, pyrometras (removing pus from uterus), enterostomies (intestinal incisions), activated sulfur mange wash, magnesium sulfate laxative (Epsom salts), thiamine (vitamin B), Istin laxative, chloral hydrate (pain reliever), prednoleucotropin (for arthritis), oxytetracycline, laparotomy (opening the stomach), and acetylpromazine (tranquilizer).

Herriot waxes strongly nostalgic and sentimental in *Every Living Thing*. The most moving tale in the text is that of the widower and poor old-age pensioner Dick Fawcett and his beloved cat, Frisk. Fawcett is dying of cancer. His life is his cat. Herriot, playing medical detective, is able to save Frisk from what appears to be a fatal disease, by deducing that the cat has been at Fawcett's narcotic medication and accidentally drugging himself. Two weeks later Herriot is at Fawcett's hospital bedside for a final visit. Fawcett misses his cat but is happy that the animal is well and being taken care of. Herriot hears the old man's last words: "Frisk . . . Frisk" (*ELT*, 102).

Herriot has nostalgic feelings from his memory of the youthful Calum, feelings mixed with recollections of his earlier days with his then young family: "I have many memories of Calum, but the one that lingers most hauntingly in my mind is of his sitting among my family, his dark eyes unfathomable as they often were, fixed on somewhere high on the wall, while his fingers coaxed that plaintive music from our little squeeze-box" (*ELT*, 122). What a charming domestic portrait!

Herriot likes to recall lost or now rarely performed crafts and the proud artisans who worked them. When Herriot arrived in Yorkshire, he tells us, "every village had its blacksmith's shop and Darrowby had several" (*ELT*, 115). Denny, the expert farrier, is presented "holding the hot shoe against the foot [of a strapping hunting horse] . . . and the smell of the smoke rising from the seared horn, the glow of the forge and the ringing bang-bang as his still sprightly father hammered the glowing metal on the anvil evoked a hundred memories of a richer past" (*ELT*, 116).

"Dear old Skeldale" (*ELT,* 156) is recalled with great fondness as Herriot remembers how happy he was that, after moving his family out, the old house would remain as the surgery for the practice. He "wondered if we could ever be as happy again as we had been here" (*ELT,* 156).

Every Living Thing could be called Herriot's *The Persistence of Memory,* as it is, with the increased distancing from recollected events, so much more a remembrance than the four previous texts. Herriot has been a pilgrim from a great city to an ancient place of ingrained pantheism, where he has found a personal nirvana. He hears and transmits the lost voices of a landed people who cared for and respected their ancient land, their beasts, their way of life, and most of all, each other. Unspokenly, they found that way of life a bridge to a spiritual world, the peaceable kingdom to which all lovers of life aspire.

Herriot ends in medias res. It is the 1950s again. The Herriots are established in High Field House. Herriot has won the love of the cat Olly and Helen's admiration for his caring patience. James and Helen are together, happy, in the middle of their long life together, and the future is bright with love, children, peace, and work.

8

James Herriot's Yorkshire

In 1979, between publishing *All Things Wise and Wonderful* and *The Lord God Made Them All,* James Alfred Wight produced *James Herriot's Yorkshire,* an extraordinarily beautiful picture book, with photos by Derry Brabbs. By this time in the minds and hearts of millions of Americans and Britons, the James Herriot persona of the loveable animal doctor was deeply associated with the county of Yorkshire in what may prove to be a timeless fashion, as Thomas Hardy is with Dorset, the "Wessex" construct of his novels, or William Faulkner is with rural Mississippi, or James Joyce is with Dublin.

Possibly because of the urging of his publishers and agents, Wight decided to practice a wee bit of personal economic determinism and cash in on the popularity of the Herriot books. The 221-page *James Herriot's Yorkshire* is about two-fifths prose, so that the text is really an extended essay. I choose to read it as an homage, an act of love, respect, and gratitude. Regardless, the artistically and commercially successful book provides interesting and lucent writing despite the fact that it is a mixture, if not a muddle, of Herriot "fact-fiction," English history, and Yorkshire geography.

Herriot's part of Yorkshire is essentially what was the North Riding of the old county before the reorganization of British counties in 1974, and it is now the county of North Yorkshire. Herriot has little professional or literary interest in either the coal country of South Yorkshire or the mills of Leeds and Bradford in West Yorkshire.

In the Postscript to the text Herriot laments that length limitations prevented him from including additional favorite locales: "I have tried to paint a picture of my Yorkshire from the Pennines to the sea, but now that I have finished I feel that I have only flicked at the canvas with my brush. Many knowledgeable people will be aghast at the omission of their favourite haunts, and I have suffered in my turn at having to leave out so many villages and the hills and streams that have warmed my heart over the years." [1]

Herriot also states in the Postscript the supposed raison d'être for what is in part a travel guidebook for both Britons and overseas visitors: "I find comfort in the thought that these words and pictures may strike a responsive chord in many who love this area and who have trodden the same paths as I have. And especially I hope I have done something for the readers of my previous books who have never seen Yorkshire. In literally thousands of letters from far corners of Britain, from America, Canada, Australia and other distant parts of the world the same phrase has recurred: 'I wish I could see the places you write about' " (*JHY*, 220).

The "oddity" of *James Herriot's Yorkshire* must be dealt with first. This oddity becomes clear when compared with other travel guidebooks written by authors identified with a particular region by the public or merely by their publishers. For example, in *Nigel Nicolson's Kent* [2] the author naturally discusses his and his family's relationship with the region speaking as himself, that is, a narrator without an obvious mask like a pseudonym. All people referred to in the text live or have lived. Herriot is of course a nom de plume. When he refers to his partner, Siegfried Farnon, he is talking about a fictionalized character, although one obviously based on a real person. Yet most characters in "pure" fiction are to a greater or lesser extent based on real people.

It all gets a trifle sticky when, for example, Helen Herriot the fictionalized character no longer lives and works in the fictionalized composite called "Darrowby," but in Thirsk, Darrowby's main model, supplemented by "Richmond, Leyburn and Middleham and a fair chunk of my own imagination" (*JHY,* 22). Farnon and Herriot have their veterinary surgery in Darrowby; Sinclair and Wight have theirs in Thirsk. In *James Herriot's Yorkshire,* Farnon and Herriot now practice in Thirsk.

While some place names are real, other places are given their fictive alter egos. Similarly, the names of people are generally disguised, supposedly for purposes of professional ethics and to protect privacy, but the reader, especially the novice, can be confused. Ultimately with characters the question is: Are all names changed or only some?

The enigma maximizes when the Herriot fan learns that there was a third partner to the practice: Frank Bingham (*JHY,* 8). Bingham is not mentioned in any of the five memoirs. He lived in a real place: the town of Leyburn. Apparently the practice had a satellite surgery near sheep country in the Pennines. He has a wife named Emmy, who is or was "charming and talented" (*JHY,* 28), and whom James liked for her "friendly teasing and her wonderful cooking" (*JHY,* 21). Herriot says that "Frank died years ago, like many good vets, in a cow byre doing a tough job," but "Siegfried, happily, is still my partner and friend" (*JHY,* 18). Are "the Binghams" portraits of real people with their real names; fictions like Siegfried, based on real people with names changed; or completely fictional characters? To add to the complication, Herriot says Bingham inspired the character of "Ewan Ross" in his books (*JHY,* 18).

Herriot goes to great pains to memorialize his colleague Frank Bingham as if to make up for excluding him from the memoirs. Bingham "had spent most of his life wandering the world, usually doing something connected with horses. He had been in the Canadian North West Mounted Police and had spent years riding the Australian rabbit fences; in fact, he had lived in the saddle most of his days and could roll a cigarette with one hand as the cowboys do in the films. He came to Britain with the Australian expeditionary force at the outbreak of the First World War and qualified as a veterinary surgeon soon after" (*JHY,* 18). Bingham was fifty-eight when Herriot first met him (*JHY,* 18) and thus some thirty years older than James. As he did with the character of Calum, Herriot valorizes the adventurous life so different from his own. However, the variety of Bingham's exotic occupations and the clichéd elements like rolling cigarettes with one hand make one think of fabrication either on the author's part or on the part of the older partner impressing or spoofing his young colleague.

Of course for passionate aficionados of the Herriot saga, there is no confusion: Herriot and the author are conterminous, the memoirs are pure autobiography, and the folks are "real-lifers."

Picture books like *James Herriot's Yorkshire* serve to make the reader feel that she or he is being given the opportunity to visit beautiful or exotic places in an armchair. The illustrations are really of two kinds: the photo images and the word images. Usually the impact of the photography is primary. In this case, however, the word pictures equal the beautiful illustrations, not only because by the time of the composition of *James Herriot's Yorkshire* the author had become such a master of his craft but equally because he chose to have his narrator historicize his narration in terms of his personal past experiences, especially those related to information he correctly anticipates his reader already has about his life and career.

For example, in the chapter entitled "Youth Hostels," in which Herriot's primary task is to describe an area in the North Yorkshire Pennines, he reminds us that as a veterinary student in Glasgow he would escape his studies "every weekend to sleep under canvas at Rosneath on the Gareloch or by a stream high on the Campsei Hills above Fintry" (*JHY,* 28). Herriot then quickly moves down the years to the late 1950s when his son introduces him to another, if less rough, way to enjoy nature: hosteling.

Jimmy, a young friend, and Herriot hike together through the dales and put up in a youth hostel in which James is not in the least uncomfortable. Herriot describes the pleasant experience and from time to time digresses. He is writing circa 1979, somewhat confusingly, about events in every decade of his life from the 1930s to the time of composition, and he recalls Frank Bingham once more (*JHY,* 28). The trio walk by Wensley church, and Herriot says: "It was in the Wensley church that I was 'married' in the British television series based on my books" (*JHY,* 30). Of course the TV wedding was filmed some twenty years after the hiking episode. Later on in the book he describes, and photos show, Thirsk church, dedicated to St. Mary Magdalene, in which "Helen" and "James" were "actually" married by "Canon Young. . . . the old gentleman shivering with cold. I think he was glad when it was over and so was I" (*JHY,* 124).

As the trek of man and boys moves on, Herriot continues his nostalgic reminiscences. They pass a pub, the Wensleydale Heifer, where Helen and James had many meals over the years including their "second wedding anniversary dinner" (*JHY,* 32). Now at the ruins of Castle Bolton, Herriot shows a deep knowledge of Yorkshire history and explains that Mary Queen of Scots was for a time imprisoned there. In juxtaposition, James remembers happy times with young Helen in the vicinity (*JHY,* 35).

When the three males reach Gunnerside Gill, they "see the massive, haunting remains of the Old Gang Mines and the smelt mills lower down . . . forlorn relics of a lost industry cupped in the silent moors" (*JHY,* 53). Herriot indicates that he is not only interested in history but also in etymology: "Gunnerside! There is a Norse name for you. 'Gunnar's pasture,' where a Viking chief herded his livestock many centuries ago. . . . Between the old Nordic days and now it was once one of the great centres of the lead mining industry. . . .

The name of the mines suggest their age, Gang being old English for road" (*JHY*, 53).

As Herriot and the lads near the northwest corner of Yorkshire, through Arkin Garth Dale, Herriot thinks back twenty years to a journey in the snow, driving to a veterinary meeting with his hard-drinking colleague Granville Bennett, and by direct reference he connects *James Herriot's Yorkshire* with *All Things Bright and Beautiful* (*JHY*, 57). References to the three memoirs previously published are frequent in *James Herriot's Yorkshire,* and Herriot also likes to connect this text to the film and TV versions. For example, the beautiful photo of the water course "Watersplash" is titled: "Watersplash, seen in the opening scene of TV's *All Creatures Great and Small.*"

The author dedicated *James Herriot's Yorkshire* to his grandchildren, Emma and Nicholas, and he speaks of gentle walks pushing Emma in her "buggy" near the family's "holiday house" in West Scrafton in Coverdale. Herriot provides descriptions, more etymology, and beautiful photos of the stone house and the local views.

Not surprisingly, Herriot has much that is personal to say about Thirsk, the town and environs in which he has spent most of his life. He takes the reader on what amounts to a walking tour of the community that contains so many of his memories and that he loves so much. We see the mill where Helen worked as a secretary in the early days of their marriage. As he drove down the street, he was always able to "catch sight of her as she bent over her desk. In my memory she is always wearing a red sweater!" (*JHY*, 119). Then there is the "little house that once was Sunnyside Nursing Home where both my children were born" (*JHY*, 119, 136). Elsewhere in the text Herriot, the proud and sentimental father, inserts individual early 1950s black and white photos of Wight's children, Rosemary and Jimmy, as he takes readers back into *All Things Wise and Wonderful* (*JHY*, 136). The revisiting of the sites in the memoirs makes *James Herriot's Yorkshire* a bridge reducing the distance between the author and the narrator as here the former has considerably reduced his masking.

When Herriot describes Richmond, Redmire, and Carperby, he does so in regard to his and Helen's working honeymoon as described in *All Creatures Great and Small,* and the text provides a photo of the lovely honeymoon hotel, The Wheatsheaf (*JHY,* 127). Herriot devotes two short but delightful chapters, "Back Window and Garden" and "Pig Sty and Yard" to the model in Thirsk for Skeldale House. The photos show a charming Victorian establishment, and Herriot informs us that Helen and he lived there for eight years (*JHY,* 138). "Pig Sty and Yard" is something of a satire of the regional book of which *James Herriot's Yorkshire* is an example. The text recounts Tristan's disastrous but very, very funny experience with pigs in *All Creatures Great and Small.* The photos of nondescript brick walls and niches have no beauty or meaning except as "Herriot ruins." Perhaps the amusing close-up, full-face photo of a mournful pig says it all: not all is charming or cute in Herriot's Yorkshire (*JHY,* 140).

The last part of *James Herriot's Yorkshire* deals with a part of the old province that Herriot never worked in but one that was often the family's vacation destination, and with an area that contains many of Herriot's World War II RAF memories: the Yorkshire North Sea coast. Herriot devotes the final three long chapters to this locale: "A Day in Captain Cook Country," "Holidays on the Coast," and "Scarborough." The photos of Whitby, the coastline, and finally the "Grand Hotel" in Scarborough, where, as described in *All Things Wise and Wonderful,* he spent six months in military training, are fine works of art depicting the characteristics of Yorkshire coastal culture and nature at the shore.

Looking structurally at *James Herriot's Yorkshire,* it is hard to imagine a more personal tour of a region, one in which the author of the text sometimes presents himself, friends, relatives, and places as they really are or were, and sometimes adopts the persona of the narrator to refer to and to continue the distancing from actual experience this adoption allows. For example, he will sometimes mention his place construct "Brawton," but he reveals in the text that it is really Harrogate that he describes in his memoirs.

For someone neither nurtured nor educated in England, Wight's knowledge of English and particularly Yorkshire history is remarkable. Just before the publication of *James Herriot's Yorkshire,* the author wrote an article on his views and observations on the many faces of England's largest county. He indicates his fascination with the "reminders, the inspiring evidence of bygone things"[3] and then proceeds to offer an accurate, informed thumbnail sketch of Yorkshire history from prehistoric times through the English Renaissance.

Herriot's description, in the chapter titled "Coverdale," of the relationship of the great noble house of Warwick to the medieval monarchy and to English history in general is interesting, concise, and accurate (*JHY,* 93–94). Elsewhere, Roman British history is well served (*JHY,* 100, 116). Herriot's chapter essay on the ancient city of York is in itself a stunningly illustrated discourse on medieval history (*JHY,* 164–69). And Herriot the writer does not neglect literary history, as, for example, in the chapter on "Coxwold and Byland Abbey" he discusses the significance of, and provides a photo of, Shandy Hall, where Laurence Sterne "lived for seven years while he was vicar of Coxwold. . . . [and] where he wrote much of *Tristam Shandy, Sentimental Journey,* and *Journal to Eliza"* (*JHY,* 152–54).

One of the most attractive sections of the book, both in terms of description and photography, is the chapter entitled "Snowbound Roads," in which the Arctic conditions that sometimes engulf the Yorkshire Pennines are vividly portrayed. Photographs of snow-covered hills, frozen rivers, and snowplows hard at work, are complemented by the author's fine prose:

I began to fancy myself so much on skis that in that terrible winter of 1947 when helicopters were dropping bread to the marooned farms in the high country, I travelled on skis to many of those places with a rucksack containing my veterinary equipment. When I was successful and was able to help an ailing sheep or cow, I have to admit I felt rather dashing. The dedicated young vet swooping over the white wastes to succor his patients. It was all right as long as it didn't start to snow again, but several times I was caught in a blizzard on those wide moors and I didn't feel dashing then. I felt very alone and frightened when I realised I had no idea where I was or in what direction I was going (JHY, 110).

James Herriot's Yorkshire has become one of the leading guidebooks to the county. On any given summer day, scores, perhaps hundreds, of visitors to Herriot County are carrying copies, trudging about, and traveling the roads and the streets of the county in cars, on foot, on bikes, and in buses, desiring to see with their own eyes the places so memorably described and evocatively photographed in this most interesting and perhaps best of popular regional studies.

As I write these words, the actor Christopher Timothy, the Herriot of the BBC's *All Creatures Great and Small*, now fifty-eight years old, and the producer David Wilkinson, have filmed and begun to market a video version of *James Herriot's Yorkshire* with James Alfred Wight, now seventy-eight, appearing in it.[4] The film is seventy-five minutes long, with Timothy starring.[5] It is aimed at the British video market and the worldwide cable market. Timothy claims that the film is "pretty faithful to the book".[6] The video will probably turn out to be an international best-seller in the travelogue category. How can it miss? The faithful are waiting.

9

The Best of James Herriot,
James Herriot's Dog Stories, and Juvenile Books

Early on in the Herriot best-seller phenomenon, Wight and his publishers, Michael Joseph in London and St. Martin's in New York, began to repackage the tales into books designed for specific but narrower markets in order to maximize revenues from the material.

The Best of James Herriot: Favourite Memories of a Country Vet, brought out in 1982, a package put together by Wight, Michael Joseph, St. Martin's, and the Reader's Digest Association, has 504 pages of text accompanied by glorious color photographs, very fine sepia-tone wash prints of events in the episodes, and margin sepia line drawings: a stunningly beautiful gift book. The text is almost entirely culled from *All Creatures Great and Small, All Things Bright and Beautiful, All Things Wise and Wonderful, James Herriot's Yorkshire,* and *The Lord God Made Them All.* Wight or his publishers or both had probably concluded that he had finished with his memoirs. Thus, the book precedes *Every Living Thing* (1992), and the "Best" may have to be reconsidered in a future "Second Best" edition.

It must be said that no one who cares deeply about animals and who has fallen under the Herriot spell can do anything

146

but embrace and treasure this book even if the reader has previously read the stories. In a way, without using actual stills from the TV series, *The Best of James Herriot* cleverly presents a visual experience that is not totally dissimilar to the video one, and it is always there on the coffee table ready for viewing. The margin drawings alone are a valuable and fascinating picture history of early twentieth-century Yorkshire agriculture, and a useful illustrated dictionary of popular English breeds of dogs. For those readers who have first experienced the Herriot saga on television, *The Best of James Herriot* may be the "best" way to be introduced to the textual experiences, although the size of the tome may be somewhat off-putting for younger readers despite the many pleasures between the boards. The book's dominant visual impact, paralleling the TV series, surely was a conscious factor in the design of the text. *The Best of James Herriot* is an example of extremely effective commercial spin-off and synergy between media.

The structure of *The Best of James Herriot* is simple but very well thought out. The text begins with a short introduction "by James Herriot," in which the "author" tells about his midlife compulsion to write down the interesting experiences and stories accumulated during his many years of veterinary practice and about how this book gave him "the chance to pick out my favourite chapters—the ones my family and I have laughed at over the years and the ones my readers have said they most enjoyed."[1] Herriot recognizes in the introduction, entitled "The Books I almost never wrote," that his personal story of friendship, love, marriage, and raising children was originally an architectonic device, encouraged by his publishers, on which to hang the veterinary episodes, but that the personal story has become an integral part of the Herriot saga. The author wisely recognizes that a great nostalgia for a contained agricultural world, a fading memory of a seeming utopia of humans and animals in symbiotic harmony, surrounds and beatifies his annals. Herriot seems entwined in the text; the author himself will "spend a little time there now and then" (*Best,* 7).

Fifty-four episodes, now titled chapters, are divided into four titled parts, the first of which is called "Early Days in Darrowby." It is the longest part, consisting of nineteen chapters from *All Creatures Great and Small,* each titled for the first time with such appellations as "Arrival at Darrowby" and "The perils of Tricki Woo." The stars of this rerun are Siegfried and the Pekinese.

Part 2, "The Vet Finds a Wife," has thirteen titled chapters, taken from *All Things Bright and Beautiful* and woven around the courtship of Helen, who was introduced in Part 1. Mr. Crump the winemaker and Gyp the barkless dog are featured.

The title of Part 3, "Memories of a Wartime Vet," puns, of course, on the fact that the veterinarian is also an RAF veteran. Thirteen chapters, extracted from *All Things Wise and Wonderful,* begin with the superb "Blossom comes home." They take the reader through Herriot's wartime service, and feature the birth of Jimmy Herriot. They end in relief with "Goodbye to the RAF."

Part 4, "Back to Darrowby," with nine chapters from *The Lord God Made Them All,* begins immediately after Herriot's postwar resumption of the practice. It features the birth of Rosie and the growing up of Jimmy, and it ends with the optimistic "Siegfried sees great things ahead."

Herriot readers who have read the first four memoirs would still be interested in owning *The Best of James Herriot* because of the ten superb "Special Features" interspersed within the text. "A wild, secluded land of dales and moors" is a color photo essay on the North Yorkshire countryside in all seasons. "The charm of towns" contains fine photographs of the major towns in North Yorkshire, from the Pennines to the North Sea. Especially appealing are the matching 1930s and present views of places in the Herriot texts. "Castles and houses in a northern landscape" shows the famous ruins of fortresses and church houses of the middle ages. "Ancient abbeys and village churches" contains color photos of the ruins of Byland, Rievaulx, Whitby, and Fountains Abbeys as well the ancient, but still functioning and intact, Lastingham, Wensley, and Aysgarth Churches.

"The country pub" shows exteriors and interiors of Yorkshire pubs in the 1930s and currently. "Human stories told in stone" is an interesting photo essay on stone ruins from Bronze Age circles and Roman roads, to nineteenth-century abandoned mines and kilns. "A farmer's world" shows ancient arms in present use. "Hand-made by country craftsmen" depicts woodcarvers, blacksmiths, wallers, rope makers, coopers, potters, and thatchers at work in past and present photos. "Nature in Herriot country" is a superb collection of plant, bird, fish, and animal drawings of Audubon quality. Alone they would be an excellent guidebook to North Yorkshire flora and fauna. Lastly, "Living traditions of work and play" shows the sports of the county and the gathering of participants and of spectators in the 1930s and currently. Ritual, sport, and farm life merge into customs "that stem . . . partly from ancient legends and rivalry" (*Best,* 465).

The Best of James Herriot, besides being a pleasurable narrative experience, is also a historical and sociological document, a sepia-tinted window into a time capsule by means of which the reader's generation sees early twentieth-century Yorkshire through the framing perspective of an aging man with an acute but sentimental memory. Like the persona James Herriot, this book is now a piece of Yorkshire and English history.

James Herriot's Dog Stories (1986), extracted, titled, and repackaged from the first four memoirs, contains forty-nine familiar stories, sometimes slightly changed from first publication. One additional story, "The Stolen Car," to make a round fifty, is a slight, five-page piece about an injured dog whose recovery is signaled by a restored ability to bark when his mistress's car is stolen.[2] It is a disappointing filler, a reject brought back.

For those readers who have read the previous four memoirs, the most interesting part of this text is the twenty-one-page introduction in which, except for a reference to "Siegfried" and "Helen," the author drops the Herriot persona. The narrator in the introduction is almost pure Wight. The main purpose of the introduction is to document the author's lifetime interest in and love of dogs. In his boyhood his Irish setter, Don, ran the Scottish hills with him (*Dog,* xi). Love of dogs, we learn, was a primary motivation for the author to attend veterinary school, and he was somewhat disappointed that his first (and only) job was in a large-animal practice. But with time the replacement of the horse with the tractor, a shrinking agricultural economy, and a steep rise in the number of household pets changed the practice until, to the delight of the old veterinarian, it became one-half dependent on dog and cat care.

Dogs have a useful function in the life of a country veterinarian. The author notes: "To a country vet like myself, whose life was spent on the roads and lanes, these dogs were very important" (*Dog,* xxv). They provided companionship in an often lonely job. The practitioner spent more time on the road than in any other activity of the practice (*Dog,* xxii).

Wight sets out to memorialize his dogs. He is justly proud to state that "all my dogs have lived into their teens" (*Dog,* xxiii). After Don of his boyhood, there was an unnamed beagle, then an unnamed mixed breed, and then came the most important dogs of his life: Hector and Dan, the dogs to whom *All Creatures Great and Small* was dedicated (*Dog,* xxiv). Hector was a Jack Russell terrier, "the soul of good nature" (*Dog,* xxiv) and a renowned stud dog. Dan, a Labrador retriever, had first belonged to son Jimmy but was left behind for Dad when Jimmy departed home to be married (*Dog,* xxv). The dogs got along famously, and the author still cherishes their memory. Subsequently, when daughter Rosie was living next door, her

Lab Polly joined the veterinarian on his car rounds (*Dog*, xxviii). They were soon joined by a border terrier, a breed the dog-loving vet had always desired, who was named Bodie after an actor-friend, Lewis Collins, who took the part of Bodie on the TV series "The Professionals." By now the author has had one or more new dogs to love.

After the story of the author's dogs, the story of Wight's veterinary college days in Glasgow is the most important subnarrative in the introduction and the most complete account of the author's professional education and training. He enrolled in Glasgow Veterinary College when that school and the profession was at nadir. The school had to beat the bushes for students, and it was impossible to flunk out, although many students, like Tristan, "studied" much longer than the usual five years. Wight finished in good time and was well prepared despite old retired practitioners (*Dog*, xv) who, as teachers, only read aloud from textbooks and sometimes could not hear the riot in their room. Another reality that the young student had to overcome was the major emphasis on the horse, a farm animal whose day had nearly passed, while small-animal work was disdained. But then, many other professions train their neophytes for the past. Wight endured and learned in the practical way by working with local practitioners and by observing animal treatment "in the real world" (*Dog*, xviii). He qualified, but, most of all, he had grown to love his work.

James Herriot's Dog Stories will have a very long publishing and reading life as a work cherished by dog lovers and often given to dog owners as a gift. Indeed it may prove to be the most popular pet book since T. S. Eliot's *Old Possum's Book of Practical Cats*.

JUVENILE BOOKS

Since 1984 Wight to date has adapted eight of his tales, each previously published in one of the memoirs, into books for preteen juveniles. The plan seems to have been to produce a beautifully illustrated book almost every year. The books have sold extremely well and have been enthusiastically received by critics of juvenile literature despite (or because of?) the fact that the rural and farm settings are alien to almost all urban children and that few American young people are familiar with such geographical terms or places such as "the Dales." What I find especially commendable about the Herriot juveniles is that the author never anthropomorphizes his animals to the soporific extent of having them talk. The beasts communicate but they do not speak. The stories remain realistic, and the readers are not written down to.

Moses the Kitten,[3] illustrated by Peter Barrett, tells the story of a freezing stray, found by Herriot; given to a farmer's wife; called Moses because, like his namesake, he was found in rushes; saved by being heated in the kitchen oven; and nursed by a sow so that the cat thinks his mother is a pig. The allegorical message of the tale is that the young have great survival potential if they can be flexible, adaptive, and nonprejudicial.

Only One Woof,[4] also illustrated by Peter Barrett, retells the story of Gyp the silent sheepdog, who finally "speaks" with a bark when, after many years, he sees his puppy playmate again. The lesson is that friendship endures and can make miracles.

The Christmas Day Kitten,[5] illustrated by Ruth Brown, brings the reader into the Yorkshire home of Mrs. Pickering, where the stray tabby Debbie regularly invites herself in to warm by the fire despite the presence of three resident basset hounds. One Christmas Day, before Debbie dies, she brings her kitten to Mrs. Pickering. The lonely woman sobs over the death of her feline friend but is rejuvenated by the new young life to care for. The hounds are as nonplussed as ever. The message for children is that loving and caring give meaning and purpose to life and that all creatures potentially can coexist in a "Peacable Kingdom." The story may also be saying, perhaps unintentionally but profoundly, that the "Peacable Kingdom" is most likely to be created in a "Queendom."

The next story is, inevitably, a horse story, and one of Herriot's most moving: *Bonny's Big Day,*[6] also illustrated by Ruth Brown. This is the story of the love of old Farmer John Skipton for his long-retired workhorse, whom he, at Herriot's suggestion, spruces up and enters in the Darrowby pet show, where Bonny wins top honors. Children learn respect for the old, who have worth for what they have done and who they now are, and that the old are not devoid of beauty. Also implied is that small-minded authority figures and bureaucrats, like the official who tries to bar Bonny because she is not a "family pet," can be overcome.

As stated earlier, the story of the old milk cow Blossom is Herriot's most memorable and poignant tale. In *Blossom Comes Home,*[7] illustrated by Ruth Brown, the twelve-year-old-cow, who has given so much milk but is now destined for the glue factory, breaks loose and with great dignity returns to her stall in the barn where contrite Farmer Dakin lets her live out her retirement in peace. This beautiful story teaches respect for all those animals who serve and sustain humans, and, more significantly, respect, appreciation, and gratitude for the old of all species.

The Market Square Dog,[8] illustrated by Ruth Brown, retells the heartstring-pulling tale of a dog who begs in the village market and is run over by a car. Herriot saves his life through surgery, but the stray is doomed to destruction until a kindly policeman ends the cliff-hanger by adopting the loveable dog for his family.

Oscar, Cat-about-Town,[9] illustrated by Ruth Brown, is the stray Helen adopted and fell in love with and who loves to go out to gatherings of humans and to community meetings. Eventually, his rightful owner claims him, and Helen is heartbroken, but James takes her to visit Oscar, and the pain of separation diminishes. The charm of the story is in the seemingly anthropomorphic eccentricity of the cat.

Another animal joins Herriot's petting zoo in *Smudge, the Little Lost Lamb,*[10] illustrated by Ruth Brown, in which a black-and-white lamb slips beneath a fence and wanders down the lane where he nearly freezes but is rescued by a little girl named Penny, who warms him back to life with her mother's hair dryer and who returns him to his owner. The story's lesson is twofold: do not stray from home, and bright kids can use intelligence and ingenuity in saving and caring for animals.

Published in 1992, *James Herriot's Treasury for Children*[11] reprints *Moses the Kitten, Only One Woof, The Christmas Day Kitten, Bonny's Big Day, Blossom Comes Home, The Market Square Dog, Oscar, Cat-about-Town*, and *Smudge, The Little Lost Lamb*. *James Herriot's Cat Stories* was published in September 1994.[12] What will be the next repackaging combination?

10

All Things Herriot

The critic Morris Dickstein has noted that "popular reading, like popular movie-going [and TV viewing], is an adjunct of the culture industry, not because this audience has no taste of its own but because it loves sequels and remakes, both to find out what happened next and, usually to see it all happen again. Popular reading is essentially rereading, the pursuit of a known quantity, a familiar experience: this is where culture and commerce meet."[1]

Herriot readers have bought and enjoyed the continuing saga because they have not wanted it to end and thus have reveled in the backing and filling and the repackaging of the episodes, while assuring through their patronage the continuance of production. These conservative, literate, mainstream readers, expecting to find pleasure, insight, comfort, and affirmation of traditional values in their received texts, have embraced Herriot for the accessibility of what C. S. Lewis calls "the whole goodness of a literary work."[2] These readers have eschewed hip, obscure, postmodern, sardonic, and sexually explicit and exploitative writing. Wight has stated the Herriot appeal much too simply: "I think the success of my books may be a backlash against some writers who are trying so hard to be sexy, to find new deviations to interest readers."[3]

Culture is a commodity. The Herriot industry has recognized that fact, of course, and it understands the geometrically

155

progressive effects of multimedia cross-fertilizing, and even inter-media selective redundancy through packaging. None of this is said in the spirit of pejoration. On the contrary, the success of the Herriot format and style, which recognizes that despite shifting horizons of subjects, values, and techniques in writing, the typical book lover (and buyer) continues to look for the old Aristotelian "stuff" in the text: plot; characterization; human interest; escape; a little wisdom; companionship; the twin catharses of laughter and tears; archetypal situations; and a passageway to compassion, which helps us to understand and accept nature's seemingly cruel passion and to simultaneously divert ourselves from it.

This is a plus for those who decry the erosion of the significance of the literary text in the acculturation of society. And the "readings" in TV and movie productions have, of course, not taken readers from the books, but brought them to the texts. Perhaps the images in the minds of the readers who later view the episodes are exchanged for those of the directors and actors, and perhaps the images in the minds of the viewers who later read the texts, are preset, but then again perhaps not. For many the text imagery remains compartmentalized, away from the film image. In the final analysis it does not seem to matter much. Ultimately, the individual reader directs his or her own production in the theater of the mind.

It seems evident to me that the Herriot saga has an enduring place in the history of late twentieth-century popular culture. The memoirs are bulletins from the theater of nostalgia, palpably magnetic through the pull of traditional narrative. Herriot holds up an artist's trick mirror, showing an image of society as it would like to be and also implying that the past is as present as this day. Herriot's house of memory contains a near utopian world, one in which mothers are always loved, fathers obeyed, marriage a sacrament, divorce a disgrace, honesty a given, and prevarication shameful. Most of all, the author inherently knows that nothing has happened unless someone writes it down. In that sense Herriot is a cultural historian as well as a chronicler of a stylized life.

The memoirs are also postimperial texts. They follow upon the end of empire for the British, and they appeal to those Americans who think of themselves as sharers of British culture and destiny. They also are an alternative to "India": a look not at the mighty in distant exotic conquest but at humble, nonbelligerent people in the outback of England and the near yesterday of grandfather memories.

The Herriot persona is a postmodern hero or antihero, self-effacing, directing his humor toward himself as Woody Allen does. Long-suffering and nonthreatening, he is without *Schadenfreude*. The character is both boy in the innermost frame of the narratives, hungering for life; and father figure in the outermost, looking back on a life well lived and much enjoyed. Ultimately, Herriot speaks from the father's place, in charge, with the power and control, as Foucault would say, of the representations. And we cannot deny him that, nor do we want to, because we want to believe in his message of the unity of life and because through his skilled use of traditional English, lightly salted with the "exotic" dialect of Yorkshire, the reader's unconsciousness is reminded that, at its best, the language tolerates tolerance. It is a good instrument for limning kindness and understanding. Herriot the father figure is neither "old fool" nor "tyrant" but benign, affectionate, loveable, and receiver of transferred affection for the paternal.

Herriot's portrayal of women reflects the limitations inherent in the patriarchal values of Wight's upbringing. His "Good Women" include dutiful wives, hard-working farm women, housekeepers, wealthy dowagers, debutantes, and rough but kind-hearted barmaids. Professional women receiving respect are few in number. The midwife who delivered his children not surprisingly gets good press. Mrs. Harbottle the secretary is portrayed as an "old battle ax." Yes, Helen does work for a while outside of the home, but it is temporary until the practice is successful enough for her to resume her housewife and motherly duties. Herriot, who prevented his daughter from pursuing the veterinary career she most wanted because he thought it to be too physically hard and too dirty for her, did come to regret that misplaced control, though she does well enough caring for the human animal. Herriot is patronizing when he means to laud women or, should I say, the female: women and cows are portrayed as having sexual, reproductive, and intuitive powers; men and bulls are portrayed as fools.

Ironically, the Herriot texts seem to be somewhat more popular with women than with men. Of course, women read more. And they may be, through nature or nurture, more affectionate toward small animals as well as toward small people. But the Herriot persona never enters into female space. He leaves his wife to go off to war when he does not have to. His greatest recreation, besides gazing at the entrancing landscape, is to engage in homosocial drinking, and women clearly are for him the "other" half of humanity.

Herriot is a professional person and a worker, one who loves his "craft," if a veterinarian would not object to that honorable appellation. Wight has made Herriot very skillful, a success, happy at his job. Herriot reminds us that all occupations have their dignity, their discourse, and their narratives. Indeed, the ultimate prompt is that all lives are intrinsically interesting.

Americans have taken Herriot to their hearts. The memoirs and the TV adaptations appear to have cut across class and cultural boundaries, appealing to the BBC–Masterpiece Theatre crowd as well as to millions of other Americans, popular culture consumers of all classes, who have pets and who love animals when they are not eating them. He has reconnected us to our archetypal herder-cultivator roots, to our literary, cultural, and for some our genetic New England ancestry, since much of what the meaning of being an American for nonminority people is rooted in the history and myths of New England farming. African-Americans, Hispanic-Americans, Asian-Americans, and other ethnic groups share the general need to be bound up in the sheaf of life and the archetypal journey we all have taken with our animal companions and our animal selves. And of course it must be recognized that the dominant culture inculcates Anglo-American collective history.

Furthermore, Herriot's old Yorkshire is an appealing, if austere, Eden without racial problems and distinctions, and the class problems and distinctions are quaint and remote for Americans. New England–Old England is a second "old country" for scores of millions of second-, third-, or fourth-generation Americans who have never set foot on English soil.

Gilbert and John Phelps believe that a premise of the Herriot stories is that because of "the pressures of an increasingly artificial daily existence, a (often unjustified) sense of superiority, or just ignorance, many people are losing touch with the animal world"[4] What may be Wight's greatest gift to readers is the intensification of feeling and concern for animals that his work fosters. He is the beasts' best friend. He has served animal life in their losing struggle with humans. In this regard he joins the compassionate company of Joy Adamson, Jane Goodall, Konrad Lorenz, and many others who have made us aware that with dominion comes responsibility and who have served animals in their unequal spatial conflict with humans. Wight can be counted with the concerned and compassionate who see how cruelly we exploit our fellow animals through factory farming, reduction of their habitat, pollution, poaching for ivory and "medicinal" parts, murdering for skins, torturing in animal "sports," humiliating in spectacles, abandoning pets, and so on. He has Herriot take up the ancient human challenge to make friends and communicate with the beasts through mutual trust.

The anatomy of James Alfred Wight, writer, shows a sharp eye, a skilled hand, and a good, large heart. He can paint Constable landscapes with words. He is wise in his knowledge that the great drama is the drama of birth, life, and death. He has succeeded in recording the lost voices of a landed people who loved and respected their ancient land, their animals, their way of life, and most of all, each other.

The Herriot construct, a kindly, reasonable veterinarian who has grown old in our hands even as we have added to our years, is a persona who, like most of us, has had little control over his life, as he bobbed on the waves of the Depression, World War II, the postwar slump, growing government control, the Cold War, mind-boggling change, and all "the ailments the flesh is heir to." He found some satisfaction and control of his life through the successful, if often dangerous, handling of beasts large and small, thus in his way mitigating the everyday powerlessness, as we all try to do in our own ways.

Wight has said, "Frankly, I don't like fame."[5] And I believe him. He is entitled to his say here:

> Professional critics have always tended to be nice but a bit condescending about my books. They regard me the same way that serious film critics look at movies by Disney. They acknowledge that my stuff sells, but manage to imply that it's all rather lightweight, not too taxing on the intellect. I agree with them, actually. It's only the Americans who seem to get very intense about my writing. They read into it all kinds of weighty, humanitarian, sociological meanings. It astonishes me, something I can't see. Not many of the villagers around here can see any of this in my books either. A local farmer once told me, "Your books are about *nawt* (the Yorkshire dialect for nothing)."[6]

He is modest, yes, but few readers can agree with his assessment.

What is left? What will remain? Is there something "permanent" here? Yes. Spirits seem destined to haunt England's agricultural north for some time to come. A young veterinarian with a loving wife and two small children is ever making his rounds, joining with his happy friends Siegfried and Tristan in the care of animals, and showing all who would look how significant a useful and decent life can be. Without that spirit the "world would be much the poorer."[7]

Chronology
Notes
Selected Bibliography
Index

Chronology

1916   James Alfred Wight, only child of John Henry and Hannah
            Bell Wight, born 3 October in Sunderland, England. Three
            weeks later family moves to Hillhead, near Glasgow, Scot-
            land.

1929   Decides on veterinary career after reading article on veteri-
            nary surgery in *Meccano Magazine.*

1930   Attending Hillhead High School, career choice reinforced
            and college goal established by lecture of Dr. Waterhouse,
            Principal of Glasgow Veterinary College.

1938   Graduates Glasglow Veterinary College. MRCVS. Com-
            mences practice in Thirsk, Yorkshire, as assistant to veteri-
            narian Donald Sinclair.

1939   Additional employment as Veterinary Inspector, Ministry of
            Agriculture, Fisheries, and Food.

1941   Marries Joan Catherine Danbury. Made partner in Sinclair
            practice.

1943   Enlists in Royal Air Force.

1944   Son Nicholas James born 13 February.

1945   Medically discharged from RAF. Resumes practice in
            Thrisk.

1949   Daughter Rosemary born 9 May.

1961   Sea voyage to Lithuania.

1963   Air trip to Turkey.

1966   Begins serious creative writing.

1970	Takes pseudonym James Herriot. *If Only They Could Talk.*
1972	*It Should Happen to a Vet. All Creatures Great and Small.*
1973	*Let Sleeping Vets Lie.*
1973–1974	President, Yorkshire Veterinarian Society.
1974	Film *All Creatures Great and Small* with Simon Ward as James and Anthony Hopkins as Siegfried. *Vet in Harness. All Things Bright and Beautiful.*
1976	*Vets Might Fly.*
1977	*Vet in a Spin. All Things Wise and Wonderful.*
1978	BBC serial commences with Christopher Timothy as James and Robert Hardy as Siegfried.
1979	Order of the British Empire, Hon. D.Litt. from Heriot-Watt University, Edinburgh. *James Herriot's Yorkshire.*
1981	*The Lord God Made Them All.*
1982	Fellow of Royal College of Veterinary Surgeons. *The Best of James Herriot.*
1983	Hon. D.V.Sc. from Liverpool University.
1984	*Moses the Kitten.*
1985	*Only One Woof.*
1986	*James Herriot's Dog Stories. The Christmas Day Kitten.*
1987	*Bonny's Big Day.*
1988	*Blossom Comes Home.*
1989	*The Market Square Dog.*
1990	*Oscar, Cat-about-Town.*
1991	*Smudge, the Little Lost Lamb.*
1992	*Every Living Thing. James Herriot's Treasury for Children.*
1994	*James Herriot's Cat Stories.*
1995	Died of cancer at his home in Thirlby, Yorkshire, 23 February.

Notes

1. THE PRINCE OF THE PEACEABLE KINGDOM

1. Timothy Green, "Best-selling Vet Practices as Usual," *Smithsonian*, Nov. 1974, 91.

2. Caroline Moorehead, "How a Country Vet Turned into a Best Seller," *London Times*, 23 July 1976, 12.

3. In William Foster, "It Shouldn't Happen to a Vet," *Saga Magazine*, Nov./Dec. 1992, 7.

4. Foster, 7.

5. James Herriot, *James Herriot's Yorkshire* (New York: St. Martin Press, 1979), 119.

6. James Herriot, "Why I love Thirsk," *Yorkshire Evening Press*, 22 Dec. 1992, 3.

7. Suzanne Del Balso, "The Wise, Wonderful, World of the Real James Herriot," *Good Housekeeping*, Mar. 1979, 180.

8. *The Lord God Made Them All* (New York: St. Martin's Press, 1981), 266–342.

9. Green, 92.

10. Green, 92.

11. Green, 92.

12. Foster, 7.

13. Moorehead, 13.

14. Del Balso, 181.

15. Del Balso, 181.

16. Stefan Kanfer, "The Marcus Welby of the Barnyard," *Time*, 29 June 1981, 78.

17. Del Balso, 148–49.

18. Gary Weiss, "The Vitinry' Is In," *Business Week,* 5 Nov. 1990, 42A.

19. Green, 94.

2. THE HERRIOT MYSTIQUE

1. Q. D. Leavis, *Fiction and the Reading Public* (London: Chatto & Windus, 1932; reprint, 1965), 214.

3. ALL CREATURES GREAT AND SMALL

1. C. S. Lewis, *An Experiment in Criticism* (Cambridge, England: Cambridge Univ. Press, 1965), 4.

2. Catherine Kelly, "Home, James," *Yorkshire Sunday,* 31 Oct. 1993, 24.

3. See Sanford Sternlicht, *Siegfried Sassoon* (New York: Twayne, 1993), 8, 15, 82–91.

4. *All Creatures Great and Small* (New York: St. Martin's Press, 1972,) 9; hereafter cited in the text as *AC.*

4. ALL THINGS BRIGHT AND BEAUTIFUL

1. Daisy Maryles, "Behind the Bestsellers," *Publishers Weekly,* 7 Sept. 1992, 16.

2. *All Things Bright and Beautiful* (New York: St. Martin's Press, 1974), 1; hereafter cited in the text as *ATBB.*

3. Wight quoted in Arturo F. Gonzalez, Jr., "James Herriot," *Saturday Review,* May 1986, 89.

4. Gonzalez, 89.

5. ALL THINGS WISE AND WONDERFUL

1. Richard R. Lingeman, "Animal Doctor," *New York Times Book Review,* 18 Sept. 1977, 13.

2. *All Things Wise and Wonderful* (New York: St. Martin's Press, 1977), 64–68; hereafter cited in the text as *ATWW.*

3. Liz Nickson, "Life Visits Herriot Country," *Life,* Mar. 1988, 67.

6. THE LORD GOD MADE THEM ALL

1. *The Lord God Made Them All* (New York: St. Martin's Press, 1981), 1; hereafter cited in the text as *LGMTA.*

2. Gonzalez, 88.

3. Henrietta Buckmaster, "Review of *The Lord God Made Them All,*" *Christian Science Monitor,* 8 June 1981, 21.

7. EVERY LIVING THING

1. *Every Living Thing* (New York: St. Martin's Press, 1992), 1; hereafter cited in the text as *ELT.*

2. Maeve Binchy, "Make Wake for Badgers," *New York Times Book Review,* 6 Sept. 1992, 6.

3. Materials provided by BBC Lionheart TV, New York.

4. Binchy, 5.

5. Stefan Kanfer, "The Marcus Welby of the Barnyard," *Time,* 29 June 1981, 14.

8. JAMES HERRIOT'S YORKSHIRE

1. *James Herriot's Yorkshire* (New York: St. Martin's Press 1979), 220; hereafter cited in the text as *JHY.*

2. *Nigel Nicolson's Kent,* photos by Patrick Sutherland (London: Weidenfeld & Nicolson, 1988).

3. "*All Things Bright and Beautiful,*" *Glasgow Herald,* 29 Sept. 1979, 9.

4. Rachel Simpson, "Animal Magnetism," *Daily Express,* 9 Dec. 1993, 50.

5. Kelly, 24.

9. THE BEST OF JAMES HERRIOT, JAMES HERRIOT'S DOG STORIES, AND JUVENILE BOOKS

1. *The Best of James Herriot* (New York: St. Martin's Press, 1983), 6; hereafter cited in the text as *Best.*

2. *James Herriot's Dog Stories,* illust. Victor G. Ambrus (New York: St. Martin's Press, 1986), 302–5; hereafter cited in the text as *Dog.*

3. *Moses the Kitten,* illust. Peter Barrett (New York: St. Martin's Press, 1984).

4. *Only One Woof,* illust. Peter Barrett (New York: St. Martin's Press, 1985).

5. *The Christmas Day Kitten,* illust. Ruth Brown (New York: St. Martin's Press, 1986).

6. *Bonny's Big Day,* illust. Ruth Brown (New York: St. Martin's Press, 1987).

7. *Blossom Comes Home,* illust. Ruth Brown (New York: St. Martin's Press, 1988).

8. *The Market Square Dog,* illust. Ruth Brown (New York: St. Martin's Press, 1989).

9. *Oscar, Cat-about-Town,* illust. Ruth Brown (New York: St. Martin's Press, 1990).

10. *Smudge, The Little Lost Lamb,* illust. by Ruth Brown (New York: St. Martin's Press, 1991).

11. *James Herriot's Treasury for Children,* illust. Ruth Brown and Peter Barrett (St. Martin's Press, 1992).

12. *James Herriot's Cat Stories,* illust. Lesley Holmes (New York: St. Martin's Press, 1994).

10. ALL THINGS HERRIOT

1. Morris Dickstein, "Damaged Literacy: The Decay of Reading," *Profession* 93 (1994): 35.

2. Lewis, 137.

3. "Interview with James Herriot," *Maclean's* 29 May 1978, 5.

4. Gilbert and John Phelps, eds. *Animals Tame and Wild* (New York: Sterling, 1979), intro.

5. *Maclean's,* 4.

6. *Maclean's,* 5.

7. Alan Bennett, "Chasing the Simple Life," *Daily Express,* 8 Feb. 1975, 9.

Selected Bibliography
James Herriot

MEMOIRS

If Only They Could Talk. London: Michael Joseph, 1970.

It Shouldn't Happen to a Vet. London: Michael Joseph, 1972.

All Creatures Great and Small (contains *If Only They Could Talk* and *It Shouldn't Happen to a Vet*). New York: St. Martin's Press, 1972; London: Michael Joseph, 1975.

Let Sleeping Vets Lie. London: Michael Joseph, 1973.

Vet in Harness. London: Michael Joseph, 1974.

All Things Bright and Beautiful (contains *Let Sleeping Vets Lie* and *Vet in Harness*). New York: St. Martin's Press, 1974; London: Michael Joseph, 1976.

Vets Might Fly. London: Michael Joseph, 1976.

Vet in a Spin. London: Michael Joseph, 1977.

All Things Wise and Wonderful (contains *Vets Might Fly* and *Vet in a Spin*). New York: St. Martin's Press, 1977; London: Michael Joseph, 1978.

James Herriot's Yorkshire. Illustrated with photographs by Derry Brabbs. London: Michael Joseph; New York: St. Martin's Press, 1979.

(With others) *Animals Tame and Wild.* Compiled by Gilbert Phelps and John Phelps. New York: Sterling Publishing Co., 1979; reprint, as *Animal Stories: Tame and Wild,* New York: Sterling Publishing Co., 1985.

The Lord God Made Them All. London: Michael Joseph; New York: St. Martin's Press, 1981.

Best of James Herriot: Favorite Memories of a Country Vet. London: Michael Joseph, 1982; published as *The Best of James Herriot,* New York: St. Martin's Press, 1983.

James Herriot's Dog Stories. Illustrated by Victor G. Ambrus. London: Michael Joseph; New York: St. Martin's Press, 1986.

Every Living Thing. London: Michael Joseph; New York: St. Martin's Press, 1992.

James Herriot's Cat Stories, Illustrated by Lesley Holmes. New York: St. Martin's Press, 1994.

JUVENILE BOOKS

Moses the Kitten. Illustrated by Peter Barrett. London: Michael Joseph; New York: St. Martin's Press, 1984.

Only One Woof. Illustrated by Peter Barrett. London: Michael Joseph; New York: St. Martin's Press, 1985.

The Christmas Day Kitten. Illustrated by Ruth Brown. London: Michael Joseph; New York: St. Martin's Press, 1986.

Bonny's Big Day. Illustrated by Ruth Brown. London: Michael Joseph; New York: St. Martin's Press, 1987.

Blossom Comes Home. Illustrated by Ruth Brown. London: Michael Joseph; New York: St. Martin's Press, 1988.

The Market Square Dog. Illustrated by Ruth Brown. London: Michael Joseph; New York: St. Martin's Press, 1989.

Oscar, Cat-about-Town. Illustrated by Ruth Brown. London: Michael Joseph; New York: St. Martin's Press, 1990.

Smudge's Day Out. Illustrated by Ruth Brown. London: Michael Joseph; Published as *Smudge, the Little Lost Lamb,* New York: St. Martin's Press, 1991.

James Herriot Storybook. Illustrated by Ruth Brown. London: Michael Joseph, 1992.

James Herriot's Treasury for Children. Illustrated by Ruth Brown and Peter Barrett. New York: St. Martin's Press, 1992.

Index